Vocation

Our Life Work

"From Grandpa With Love"

Copyright © 2015 Marvin J. Martin
All rights reserved.

ISBN: 1502585529
ISBN 13: 9781502585523
Library of Congress Control Number: 2014917729
CreateSpace Independent Publishing Platform
North Charleston, South Carolina

If you find the information beneficial, and you want to pass it on to others, permission is given to reproduce this book, provided the copies are complete, unaltered, and unabridged, including this copyright page, and circulated free of charge.

Unless otherwise noted, Scripture taken from the HOLY BIBLE, NEW INTERNATIONAL VERSION ® Copyright © 1973, 1978, 1984 by International Bible Society. Used by permission of Zondervan Publishing House. All rights reserved.

The "NIV" and "New International Version" trademarks are registered in the United States Patent and Trademark Office by the International Bible Society. Use of either trademark requires the written permission of International Bible Society.

A Collection of Later in Life Writings

"From Grandpa With Love"

Volume IV

Whatever you do, work at it with all your heart, working for the Lord, not for men, since you know you will receive an inheritance from the Lord as a reward. It is the Lord Christ you are serving.
(Colossians 3:23–24)

Vocation

This is the fourth in a series of five *"From Grandpa With Love"* books that consolidate for publication many of the booklets I have been writing over the past thirty-five years to pass on what God was teaching me about life.

We opened the series with an overview of life entitled, *Four Generations: A Journey Through Life*. The next three volumes (*Faith, Marriage,* and *Vocation*) deal with a trio of lifetime decisions we discussed briefly in *Four Generations* as follows:

> As I look back across my life, I see three principal lifetime decisions and three important decision times...The three decisions concern our *Faith*, our *Marriage*, and our *Vocation*. Some have referred to these as our *Master*, our *Mate*, and our *Mission*. The three decision times usually seem to occur toward the end of each generation as we prepare to enter the next season of our lives.

Vocation

The series concludes with *Passing It On*, discussing the age-old opportunity we have to invest in others what we have experienced and learned during our own journeys.

Once more I say, "*Thank You.*" How grateful I am to the Lord and all those He has used to teach me, help me, and contribute to whatever I have written.

To God Be the Glory!

From Grandpa With Love

Marvin J. Martin
Wichita, Kansas
2015

Contents

Prologue		vii
Part I	Trying To Do Right	1
Part II	Resolving Disputes and Avoiding Litigation	25
Part III	Harmony in the Work Place	51
Part IV	Working With Words	145
Part V	Ministering Free of Charge	155
Epilogue	Chasing the Wind!	173

Prologue

In *Four Generations*, the first book in our series, we twice discussed the subject of *Vocation*: first, in Age 21–25 as we were beginning to make *Lifetime Decisions* about our life work; and later, toward the end of life in Age 65–70 as we contemplated *Passing the Baton* to those who are following.

Since the material in the rest of this book on *Vocation* will talk about some of the specific ways God's call on my life was lived out, I thought it would be good to review this earlier material before we move on.

Age 21–25. Lifetime Decisions
Our vocation is our "calling," or "voca" (the root word for "vocal"). Unfortunately, there may be a great difference between our calling from God and the job we perform in the workplace. Someone has divided them into Empire building for this world and Kingdom building for eternity. Most of our years of schooling are directed toward making us proficient in our worldly trade, business or profession, and virtually none is directed toward hearing and responding to the call of God.

How I would have profited from hearing early in life the words of Ephesians 2:10:

> *For we are God's workmanship, created in Christ Jesus to do good works, which God prepared in advance for us to do.*

How much it would mean for us to know during our growing up years that God has made us perfect for the work He created for us to do, and that our role is to listen for His call and then to respond, *"Here am I. Send me!"*

I entered the field of law because I was a word person and others I respected encouraged me in that direction. I enjoyed the study of law. I readily understood it was a good and honorable profession that could do good in this world; but I did not see nor understand until many years later how it might be used to build God's Kingdom.

There is a thrill in studying intensely and finally receiving an advanced degree. But I have found it is nothing compared to the thrill and fulfillment of being called and prepared by God to use this knowledge and degree and everything else God has given us to help in the building of His Kingdom rather than worldly Empires!

I think Peter experienced this when he first met Jesus, shortly after Peter had finished an unsuccessful night of fishing. Jesus first demonstrated His control of worldly success by telling Peter where to throw his nets for a record catch, so large the nets began to break and the boats began to sink; then he immediately invited Peter and his brother Andrew to leave it all:

"Come, follow me," Jesus said,
"and I will make you fishers of men."
(Matthew 4:19)

A short time ago one of my sons startled me with the question. "Your work wasn't all that important to you, was it?" After practicing law, which I thoroughly enjoyed, for over forty years, I at first started to insist that he was wrong. But as I slowly reflected, I finally responded, "You're right. It was the people and God's word that have been important." My work was, of course, very important, *at that time,* as a building block God was using in my life. But it was *not the major purpose in life* that I felt it to be at the time.

I am convinced that we need to work to survive in this world (2 Thessalonians 3:10), but I have also discovered that we need to keep this world and eternity in proper perspective.

As Paul instructs his young protégé, Timothy:

> *For physical training is of some value,*
> *but godliness has value for all things,*
> *holding promise for both the present life*
> *and the life to come.*
> (I Timothy 4:8)

In other words, this world is important but it is only part of eternity. Therefore, I have concluded we need to prepare and then major in Kingdom building and not just our secular work. When we do that, Jesus assures us He will see that all our physical needs are met:

> *But seek first his kingdom and his righteousness,*
> *and all these things* [i.e. worldly needs]
> *will be given to you as well.*
> (Matthew 6:33)

***

Vocation

Now let's look at the conclusions I reached as I looked back in the autumn of life.

***

Age 65–70 Passing the Baton
For many years I did not sufficiently appreciate the difference between our vocation and our job or profession. The world interchanges these terms and so did I. Gradually, however, I began to see that our vocation, or what I now often refer to as our "voca," as in "vocal," is actually our "calling" from God. By contrast I believe our job or profession is the way we financially support ourselves, and *one* place where we carry out our vocations. Thus, if my *calling* is to *bring harmony,* then I do it in my job or profession but I also do it at home, at church, and in the community. It's much like the distinction between "transportation" and "railroads" or "airlines." The latter two are simply tools to help accomplish the former. So, too, jobs and professions, I believe, are merely tools to help us carry out the broader calling we receive from God.

The apostle, Paul, understood this distinction. Sometimes he supported himself as a tentmaker (Acts 18:3 and 2 Thessalonians 3:7–10); sometimes he was supported by other churches (2 Corinthians 11:8); and sometimes he was supported by the state—as a prisoner! (1 Corinthians 11:23). The *method* of financial support, which today we would refer to as his job or profession, often changed, but the *message* of the gospel never varied, as he carried out his calling from God described in Acts 26:17–18:

Prologue

> *I will rescue you from your own people and from the Gentiles.*
> *I am sending you to them to open their eyes*
> *and turn them from darkness to light,*
> *and from the power of Satan to God,*
> *so that they may receive forgiveness of sins*
> *and a place among those who are sanctified by faith in me.*

Regardless of his job or method of support, Paul never wavered from this original calling from God. (Acts 26:19–29; Colossians 1:24–29)

Like Paul, we are to carry out the commission or calling God gives to us, regardless of circumstances. Age, health, or other factors may cause us to retire from our job or our profession, but not from our vocation. We are still to be about God's business, in whatever way he calls us to serve, even though we may now be financially supported by pensions or savings rather than by salaries or other earned income.

I believe our call, or at least the emphasis of our call, may change as we move through life. But I don't think we abolish or abandon what we were doing as much as we build on it. The work we have done at each stage of life has been important in its time. But now as we retire, we have the opportunity to build on our early years and experiences to complete the final work God has for us in these later years. As one wise older man told me, "Don't do something entirely new after you retire; instead, hone what you worked on earlier." Like Peter, we don't stop being fishermen; rather, we can now concentrate on being fishers of *men*, without having also to concern ourselves with catching *fish!* (Luke 5:1–11).

Vocation

***

With that background in mind, I invite you to look at the following booklets and other material that I wrote over the years as I merged my calling from God (my vocation), with my responsibilities and activities her on earth. Your life will be unique and different from mine, but hopefully one older man's experiences and conclusions will help you in your journey.

As always, remember that we all err. So hold onto what is good (of God)—and discard the rest.

From Grandpa With Love

Part I
Trying to Do Right

Whatever you do, work at it with all your heart, working for the Lord, not for men, since you know you will receive an inheritance from the Lord as a reward. It is the Lord Christ you are serving.
(Colossians 3:23–24)

Preface
1992

This booklet was given to those who attended a Rotary meeting I had been asked to address as a practicing lawyer in my hometown. Over the years, the talk was repeated several times and the booklets were distributed to others.

Although circumstances and laws change with the passage of time, the core message in the following pages still seems appropriate. Hopefully, it will be of value to those who read it in their time and place.

From Grandpa With Love

Trying to Do Right

Introduction

Several years ago, I attended a funeral I have never forgotten. After the pastor finished the eulogy, he stepped away from the pulpit, sat down at the piano, and began to sing a very touching song. I can still hear his deep bass voice singing the refrain over and over again:

"Oh Lord—I Tried!"

That was over thirty years ago. I've never heard the song again, but I've never forgotten those words.

I believe most of us, if we were asked, would say that we, too, are trying—trying to do right! I'm sure that has always been difficult. But it seems especially hard today. In our fast-changing, pluralistic society, with its multiple ethnic groups, varying traditions, religions, and objectives, mixed with the current anything-goes philosophy, it often seems confused and unclear as to what "right" really is.

I suggest that there are three subjects we need to explore if we are to reach our goal of trying to do right. These subjects are **Law**, **Ethics**, and **Truth**.

I. Law
Laws are the enforceable rules by which institutions (including not only civil government but also the other three institutions of family, church, and business) govern their activities.

Laws provide the order that we need to live together. Properly used, the law is one of man's great blessings. It is the rule of law, which allows us to sleep peacefully in our homes at night, to travel in an orderly way over busy streets and highways, and to engage in much of life as we know it.

Although the law is necessary to keep order, it is also *a*-moral. It is neither right nor wrong in and of itself. It is simply force, which can be used for good or for evil. It is like nuclear energy, which can be used to light up or to blow up a city.

Laws vary from place to place. In the United States, local laws are different from city to city and from state to state. What is legal in Kansas may not be legal in Oklahoma. Laws vary even more from country to country. For example, it may be legal in one nation to cut off the hand of a thief, but in another country the officer attempting to enforce such punishment would himself be subject to arrest and prosecution.

Laws also change from time to time. The law reflects the mores and moral codes of those in power at any given time. It is a changing, ever-evolving set of rules by which society is governed. To illustrate this principle, let me give you three examples of changes in the law, which have occurred since I began practicing law in early 1951.

The first example is found in the area of equal rights. In 1896, the US Supreme Court held that "separate but equal" facilities for blacks and whites, was the law.[1] However, in 1954, the same Supreme Court (by then composed of nine different justices) determined that "separate is inherently unequal" and dramatically changed the entire course of US law (and social ethic) by one momentous decision.[2]

A second illustration is cohabitation without marriage. When I began the practice of law, cohabitation without marriage was considered a crime in many jurisdictions.[3] By contrast today, such practice is commonplace and widely accepted.

As a final example, let's look briefly at the issue of abortion, which is being so hotly contested today. At the time I started the practice of law, a medical doctor who committed an abortion (except for very narrow legally permissible grounds) would probably have lost his license and been charged with a felony.[4] Today, the government, which might formerly have removed the doctor's license and imprisoned him for commission of such an abortion, may pay his fee for performing the act.[5]

Obviously, it isn't *justice* or *fairness* or *right* or *wrong*, which have changed. Instead, those persons now in power have views that differ from the views of preceding generations concerning the propriety of such issues as race, marriage, and abortion, and they have changed "the law" to fit their interpretation of what is just and fair and right and wrong.

We need laws for order and security. However, the fact that laws vary from place to place and change from time to time shows us that we do not necessarily "do right" simply by following the law. We need something more.

II. Ethics

Some believe that what we need to "do right" is to establish and abide by agreed-upon codes of ethics. Even though ethics is a very popular subject today, most of us have a hard time understanding just what it is, as illustrated by the following joke now circulating:

> "What are ethics, Dad?" a small boy asked his father. The father, who owned a small business, answered: "Let me give you an example. Do you remember old Mrs. Jones who trades with us?" The son replied, "Yes, why?" The father continued. "Well, a few days ago, she came in to pay her account with us. She gave me a twenty-dollar bill, and I gave her change. After she left, I discovered she had given me two twenty-dollar bills stuck together. Now ethics, son, is this: Shall I, or shall I not, tell my partner about the extra twenty dollars?"

Despite such stories, we generally think of ethics as society's *ideal* for conduct. Ethics can be defined as a set of principles of right and wrong. Thus, where *law* deals with the enforceable rules of a group, *ethics* deals with a group's principles concerning right and wrong.

As our culture has changed through technology, internationalization, intermingling of values, and the changing roles of women, minorities, the disabled, and other groups, our composite view of ethics, i.e., right and wrong, has also changed. Today, we find ourselves writing massive ethical codes for government, businesses, and other institutions as we try desperately to have our ideals of right and wrong keep pace with our rapidly changing society.

Recently, as a group of us discussed this subject, we asked those in attendance to vote on the following question:

> "Is it ethical or unethical for an individual to buy box seats and expensive dinners for those who place orders for the individual's best customers?"

In other words, was such a practice ethical sales promotion or was it an unethical practice akin to bribery? About two-thirds of those present voted that the practice of "promoting" sales through such gifts was ethical. One-third of the group voted that it was unethical. We concluded, therefore, that since the cultural ethic of a group in our society was set by the majority, the practice of expensive sales promotions was ethical *for that particular group*.

Interestingly, however, some of those in attendance noted that many companies, especially those with defense contracts, will not allow any gift to be accepted or given in order to avoid criticism or violation of laws.

This simply underscores again that ethics, like law, varies from time to time and from place to place and, while it is an aid to better conduct, it does not always provide a firm standard of right and wrong.

III. Truth
Since both laws and ethical standards vary from place to place, change from time to time, and are subject to error, we find ourselves still asking, "How can we succeed in our quest of 'trying to

do right'?" Every time we are faced with a decision, we consciously or subconsciously ask ourselves this question. Sometimes, it is a simple, everyday issue, e.g.,

- "What is the right amount to charge for our products and services?"
- "Who is the right person to vote for?"
- "What is the right amount to give to a charity?"
- "What is the right discipline and reward for our children and others for whom we are responsible?"

Occasionally, however, it involves life or death, e.g.,

"When, if ever, do we have the right to terminate the life of an unborn child or an aged, chronically ill loved one?"

It is at times like these that we empathize deeply with Pilate who, as he struggled with whether to free Jesus or to crucify Him, finally cried out in frustration, "What is truth?"[6]

While abiding by the law of a particular government or other institution may bring order and the approval of those in authority, and abiding by the ethical standards of our peers may bring us the approval of a majority of that particular group, neither of these will assure that we are *doing right*. We can only be sure that we are doing what is *truly right* when we know and abide by the *truth*.

How, then, do we answer this haunting question:

"What is truth?"

Truth is reality. It is what is. It is an infinite and omniscient view of life and how it should be lived. Truth is perfect. It is eternal. It never changes. Truth is the same everywhere. It brings harmony and order. It does not bring about bad, but good. Truth is always reliable.

But where do we find this truth? If we cannot always trust the laws of those in authority over us, nor the ethical standards of our peers around us, to whom or to what do we look to give us this perfect, eternal, unchanging, reliable truth?

Every individual and group must ultimately face his or her own moment of truth. For me, this occurred during the chaotic years of the 1960s and 1970s. When I realized that there was no certainty in laws and standards of ethics, which changed with the times, places, and persons involved, I was deeply troubled. I was a lawyer, husband, and father. How was I to carry out my roles and responsibilities in a world of changing values, traditions, and morals? Buildings were being burned and public figures assassinated; women's roles were topsy-turvy as they were moving out into the work world; promiscuity was rampant; our nation was at war with itself over an unpopular, undeclared war in Southeast Asia; a presidency was in jeopardy over Watergate; economics was in crisis as inflation soared worldwide and business integrity seemed to be crumbling.

Out of desperation, I turned to the Bible. Not for an intellectual exercise, but for real answers. To find out what was *really* right—what was unchanging, always reliable and *true*.

Through this Book, God gradually began to reveal His answers. It was His truth, which had remained constant and unchanging for thousands of years that began to set me free. In the Bible I found that there was a reliable basis for all of life, including stable and enduring marriages and families; help in resolving disputes and avoiding litigation in an increasingly litigious society; aid in choosing and enjoying a life work; and an eternal view of time and the chapters of life.

But as I probed deeper over the years, I have come to realize that Biblical truth is a common heritage for all of us who live in this wonderful country!

While we are now becoming a multicultural society, which seems to be fragmenting and somewhat directionless (or more accurately, being pulled in many directions by many traditions and cultures), there is no denying that historically both the Law and Ethic in the United States have come from a belief in God and the teachings of the Bible. It is God and the Bible, which have been the traditional source of truth in our society. For example, when witnesses in the United States have been called to testify in court proceedings, they have historically placed their hands on the Bible, and they have been asked, "Do you solemnly swear to tell the truth, the whole truth, and nothing but the truth, so help you God?" or words of similar import.[7]

Much of our civil and criminal laws can trace their origins to biblical roots. Items such as murder, manslaughter, theft, contracts, divorce, and punitive damages are all discussed at length in the Scriptures.

And it is not only our laws, but also our entire ethical culture, which has been permeated by the principles of both the Old and New Testaments. The wisdom of Solomon, the Good Samaritan, and principles such as the Golden Rule form a bedrock for the ethical values of our nation.

Take, for example, the Rotary Four Way Test, one of the most widely known codes of ethics in force today. This Four Way Test opens with the question we are considering today, "Is it the truth?" and then adds, "Is it fair to all concerned? Will it build good will and better friendships? Will it be beneficial to all concerned?"

Herbert J. Taylor wrote this code of ethics in 1932 while he was president of a struggling cooking utensil firm in Oklahoma. Taylor's own individual conscience was deeply marked by the Scriptures, and he reportedly memorized and recited each day the Sermon on the Mount. In 1954, while Taylor was President of Rotary International, he made the Four Way Test available to this organization. Today, over a million Rotarians worldwide have a higher ethical standard because of the influence of this strong follower of Christ.[8]

The impact of religion upon our laws and ethics began with the earliest explorers and has continued to this day.

1492
For example, Christopher Columbus, in describing his first trip to the New World in 1492, said:

"I set forth in the name of the Holy Trinity...And in a little while I say that, not by [my own might], but by the grace of God, I discovered three hundred and thirty-three leagues of Tierra Firme..."[9]

1620

The Pilgrims who landed in New England in 1620 to plant the first colony in that area of the New World, established their form of government and signed the document now known as the Mayflower Compact in which their trust in God and their desire to advance the Christian faith was set forth:

> In the name of God, Amen. We whose names are underwritten, the loyal subjects of our dread sovereign Lord King James, by the grace of God, of Great Britain, France and Ireland, King, Defender of the Faith, et al, having undertaken for the glory of God, and the advancement of the Christian faith, and honor of our king and country, a voyage to plant the first colony in the northern parts of Virginia, do by these presents solemnly and mutually in the presence of God and of one another, covenant and combine ourselves in a civil body politic...[10]

1776

The Declaration of Independence, which was drafted in 1776 clearly reflects our forefathers' conviction about God and truth as it states:

> We hold these truths to be self-evident, that all men are created equal, that they are endowed by their Creator with certain unalienable rights...[11]

1861

The Kansas constitution, adopted in 1861, like the constitutions of most other states, begins with a public dependence upon God:

> We, the people of Kansas, grateful to Almighty God for our civil and religious privileges, in order to ensure the full enjoyment of our rights as American citizens, do ordain and establish this constitution of the State of Kansas...[12]

1892

In 1892, the US Supreme Court, after reciting four hundred years of our religious history in a case it was deciding, concluded:

> ...There is no dissonance in these declarations. There is a universal language pervading them all, having one meaning. They affirm and reaffirm that this is a religious nation.[13]

1992

Our deep dependence upon God has been publicly continued by many of our leaders down to the present time. For example, President Bush, following the tradition of many presidents before him, affirmed this fact in his 1991 Thanksgiving Day Proclamation, which opened with these words:

> From the moment it was 'conceived in liberty and dedicated to the proposition that all men are created equal,' our Nation has enjoyed the mercy and protection of Almighty God.

Notwithstanding our long history, there has been unleashed in recent years a broadscale effort, which seems designed to remove God from public expression. We are being increasingly told that religion is a private matter, and that it is improper to speak or acknowledge our dependence upon God in the public arena. For example:

- The US Supreme Court has ordered that school children may no longer have open prayer nor reverent Bible reading in government funded schools.[14]
- A federal appeals court has decided that a public school teacher cannot keep a Bible on his desk.[15]
- A judge has been stopped from opening his court with prayer.[16]
- A public university professor has been ordered not to disclose his personal religious views to his students during class time.[17]
- The Ten Commandments can no longer be posted in public schools.[18]
- Those who mention God in public graduation ceremonies are criticized.[19]
- The motto "In God We Trust" seems condoned because it is a tradition rather than because it is a statement of faith.[20]

As we publicly separate ourselves from God and act independently of His moral principles, our nation has become increasingly imperiled. We now have many in positions of leadership and authority who have turned away from God and the institutions of the family, the church, and business, and are increasingly asking and expecting the one institution of government to solve all problems. At the same time, they attempt to expunge God and many of His principles from this final institution.

Vocation

I submit to you that it will not work. The basis for law, order, peace, security, and prosperity of any nation is an underlying dependence upon God. This is not an option.

As George Washington stated in his first Thanksgiving Proclamation in 1789:

> It is the duty of all nations to acknowledge the providence of Almighty God, to obey His will, to be grateful for His benefits and humbly to implore His protection and favor.[21]

The primary purpose of both laws and ethics is to protect mankind from itself. Both the Old and New Testaments inalterably link the proper treatment of our fellow man with public acknowledgement and respect for God. A paraphrase of the first four of the Ten Commandments tells us that we are commanded to put God first, not to worship false idols, not to take His name in vain, and to keep the Sabbath holy. It is only when we acknowledge our Creator and obey His commands that we treat His world and His creatures properly. When we have a proper respect for God, we also tend to respect other people by trying to abide by the last six of these commandments by honoring our father and mother, and by not murdering, not committing adultery, not stealing, not bearing false witness, and not coveting what our neighbors have.[22]

The New Testament is even more succinct as it couples these same two concepts of respect for God with proper treatment of our fellow man as it sets forth what has become known as the Great Commandment:

"Love the Lord your God with all your heart and with all your soul and with all your strength and with all your mind"; and, "Love your neighbor as yourself."[23]

We cannot have the benefit of the principles of a Godly society without upholding God publicly. When we attempt to expunge God from our public vocabulary, but then expect people to follow His principles, we expect too much. Proof of this can be seen by looking briefly at three critical examples, which show how our society has fared in recent years as we have increasingly charted our own course rather than relying on the following timeless principles of God:

Debt
The Old Testament warned the early Israelites if they followed Him their nation would lend; and if they failed to follow Him they would become borrowers; and that the lender would control the borrower.[24] We have become a nation of borrowers. Our current economic crisis is clearly apparent from the multitrillion dollar private, corporate, and governmental debt structures, which have been used to spark the economy in the past and which are now approaching the point of no return.

Sex
Recognizing that society cannot succeed without strong, committed families, the Bible restricts sex to marriage.[25] Many now openly flaunt this tradition and cohabit without marriage in both heterosexual and homosexual relationships. The media and government are constantly discussing incest, rape, gangs, violence, and malfunctioning family units. They give lip service

Vocation

to the concept of a family, but seldom to commitment, sexual purity, and other biblical principles that make such families functional.

Dependency

- The inaugural addresses of all Presidents have made reference to God.
- The oath of President of the United States is taken by the President with his hand on the Bible.
- Every session of Congress opens with a prayer.
- A small room in the Capitol just off the Rotunda is available for private prayer and meditation of congressional members. It contains a stained glass window showing George Washington kneeling in prayer and the words from Psalm 16:1, "Preserve me, O God, for in Thee do I put my trust."
- In the Rotunda of the Capitol is a picture of the Pilgrims about to embark from Holland on the sail of which is their motto, "In God we trust, God with us."
- The phrase, "In God we trust," sits opposite the President of the Senate and is inscribed in the House of Representatives.
- In the Supreme Court building, the Ten Commandments are displayed on the wall. For many years, each session of the Court has opened with the words, "God save the United States and the Honorable Court."
- On the top of the Washington Monument are the words, "Praise be to God."
- Quotations from Scripture appear in the Library of Congress building, such as, "What doth the Lord require

of thee but to do justly and to love mercy and to walk humbly with thy God" (Micah 6:8).

- The Lincoln Memorial sets forth the words of Lincoln at the end of the Gettysburg address, "That this nation, under God, shall have a new birth of freedom, and that government of the people, by the people, for the people shall not perish from the earth." (This same declaration that we are a "nation under God" also appears in our Pledge of Allegiance, which is recited regularly by millions of our people.)
- Jefferson's words appear on his memorial: "God Who gave us life gave us liberty. Can the liberties of a nation be secure when we have removed a conviction that these liberties are the gift of God? Indeed, I tremble for my country when I reflect that God is just, that His justice cannot sleep forever."

Conclusion

What, then, is our conclusion? It is simply this: Laws and Ethics are very necessary and important as we "try to do right." We need to know and abide by these standards unless they violate our individual consciences. But most important of all we need to know and to declare publicly our dependence upon God and His Truth, so that the laws we make and the codes of ethics we attempt to follow will also be right and true.

As we try to do right, we have to be overwhelmed with a deep sense of gratitude for the past. For God and His goodness to us as a people and for our debt to our forebears who were willing not only privately, but publicly to state their dependence upon God on their money and in their written instruments, their inscriptions upon buildings, and their public proclamations, which we now draw upon for strength and support.

But we must also be grateful for the present—for members of this generation who are faithfully and sincerely acknowledging the presence and sovereignty of God in the affairs of all mankind, and endeavoring to live according to His principles. Such actions encourage us also, as we try to do right in our sphere of influence.

It is tempting to believe it was easy for a Pilgrim or George Washington, or Abraham Lincoln, but difficult for us, publicly to proclaim and to follow God. I doubt that. I suspect that many of those who publicly proclaim God in any generation may be subject to ridicule or even persecution. It is for that reason that we have grateful hearts for a country where the President can and will acknowledge Almighty God publicly and without embarrassment in a Thanksgiving Day Proclamation to the American people, even at a time when the Supreme Court is considering a case in which the lower court has held that the mention of God by a speaker in a secondary school commencement ceremony was unlawful.[26]

Finally, we can and should give thanks for the future. As I prepared this material and read various bits of information, I came across the last verse of "The Star Spangled Banner." As I read it, I realized it publicly reiterates our dependence upon God and the blessings that can come in the future when and if we try to do right by following Him.

Let's close by reading this final stanza of our National Anthem (emphasis added).

> *Blessed with victory and peace, may this* **heav'n-rescued** *land*
> **Praise the power** *that hath made and preserved us a nation!*
> *Then conquer we must, when our cause it is just;*
> *And this be our motto:*
> *"In God is our trust!"*
> *And the star-spangled banner in triumph shall waive*
> *O'er the land of the free, and the home of the brave.*

God Bless You All!

Vocation

1. Plessy v. Ferguson, 163 U.S. 537 (1896).
2. Brown v. Board of Education, 347 U.S. 483 (1954).
3. **See, e.g.,** State v. Ling, 91 Kan. 647, 138 P. 582 (1914) (1909 Kans.Gen.Stat. §2718)
4. **See, e.g.,** State v. Rudman, 126 Me. 177, 136 A. 817 (1927); In re Buck's License, 192 Or. 66, 232 P.2d 791 (1951).
5. See Medical Assistance (Medicaid) program of Title XIX of the Social Security Act, 42 U.S.C. Sections 1396 et seq.
6. John 18:38. Scripture taken from the Holy Bible, New International Version, © 1973, 1978, 1984, International Bible Society. Used by permission of Zondervan Bible Publishers.
7. Kan.Stat.Ann. §§54-102 & 104 (1991). (Note: K.S.A. §54-103 provides for "affirmation" in place of "oath" for those with conscientious scruples.)
8. The Herbert J. Taylor Story, Taylor, Herbert J., Intervarsity Press.
9. Christopher Columbus—The Motive Behind the Mission, p.7, Decision Magazine, Jan. 1992.
10. Rector of Holy Trinity Church v. United States, 143 U.S. 457 (1892).
11. Id.
12. Preamble, Kansas Constitution.
13. Rector of Holy Trinity Church v. United States, **supra**.
14. Engel v. Vitale, 370 U.S. 421 (1962). Abington v. Schempp, 374 U.S. 203 (1963).
15. Roberts v. Madigan, 921 F.2d 1047 (10th Cir., 1990), **petition for cert. filed,** (Mar. 15, 1991) (No. 90-1448).
16. North Carolina Civil Liberties Union Legal Foundation v. Constangy, 947 F.2d 1145 (4th Cir., 1991).
17. Bishop v. Aronov, 926 F.2d 1066 (11th Cir., 1991), **petition for cert. filed**, (Aug. 14, 1991) (No. 91-286).

18. Stone v. Graham, 449 U.S. 39 (1980).
19. Weisman v. Lee, 908 F.2d 1090 (1st Cir., 1990), **cert. granted sub nom**. Lee v. Weisman, 111 S.Ct. 1305 (March 18, 1991).
20. Aronov v. United States, 432 F.2d 242 (9th Cir., 1970).
21. Quoted in 1990 Thanksgiving Day Proclamation by the President of the United States.
22. Exodus 20:1–17. Scripture taken from the Holy Bible, New International Version, © 1973, 1978, 1984, International Bible Society. Used by permission of Zondervan Bible Publishers.
23. Luke 10:27. Scripture taken from the Holy Bible, New International Version, © 1973, 1978, 1984, International Bible Society. Used by permission of Zondervan Bible Publishers.
24. **See, e.g.**, Deuteronomy 28:12, 44 and Proverbs 22:7.
25. **See, e.g.**, Chapter 5 of Proverbs and 1 Corinthians 6:9–10.
26. Weisman v. Lee, **supra**.

Part II

Resolving Disputes and Avoiding Litigation

What causes fights and quarrels among you? Don't they come from your desires that battle within you? You want something but don't get it. You kill and covet, but you cannot have what you want. You quarrel and fight. You do not have, because you do not ask God.
(James 4:1–2)

Preface

2006

This booklet was first published many years ago while I was practicing law. At that time it was entitled:

*How Can Christians Help
Resolve Disputes and Avoid Litigation?*

and it began with this introductory statement:

The purpose of this booklet is to help integrate the Bible into common life. It is written from a layman's viewpoint, based on the premise that God's Word has answers for the questions of every generation. May it strengthen and refresh you and encourage you to walk ever more closely with Him.

Times have changed during the intervening years, but people have not. We still face the same fundamental human problems, and the Bible still has the same fundamental answers.

So, with the exception of a fresh title and a few editing items, the booklet is being republished in the hope it will be helpful to a new group of readers.

As always, remember we all err. So hold onto whatever is good (of God)—and discard the rest.

From Grandpa With Love

Resolving Disputes and Avoiding Litigation

Introduction

The Bible is a very practical book. It gives unchanging guidance for our daily lives. It is God's wisdom for every generation. Immediately before James poses the two questions listed above, he compares Godly wisdom with earthly wisdom, and the results of each as follows:

> *Who is wise and understanding among you?*
> *Let him show it by his good life, by deeds done in the humility*
> *that comes from wisdom. But if you harbor bitter envy and selfish*
> *ambition in your hearts, do not boast about it or deny the truth. Such*
> *'wisdom' does not come down from heaven but is earthly, unspiritual, of*
> *the devil. For where you have envy and*
> *selfish ambition, there you find disorder and every evil practice.*
> *But the wisdom that comes from heaven is first of all pure;*
> *then peace loving, considerate, submissive, full of mercy and good fruit,*
> *impartial and sincere. Peacemakers who sow in peace*
> *raise a harvest of righteousness.*
> (James 3:13–18)

Sadly, in our generation, we are increasingly applying "earthly wisdom" and thereby experiencing disputes and litigation in our marriages, our churches, our businesses, and our government. Many of these "fights and quarrels" could be resolved or avoided if we would live our lives based upon Biblical principles rather than upon earthly tradition and the advice of worldly peers.

Set forth below are ten questions with some Biblical discussions and applications, together with some concluding remarks that may help us reverse this trend. They do not contain all the answers—but hopefully, they can form a starting place to encourage us to live our lives on God's principles so we can glorify and enjoy Him and help others in our sphere of influence to do the same.

1. **What About Vows?**
Broken vows (promises) are a prime source of conflict. Not only do broken wedding vows often end in divorce court, but also many other lawsuits occur because one side or the other fails to keep its word. We should be careful, therefore, to keep our vows. As the writer of Ecclesiastes states:

> *When you make a vow to God, do not delay in fulfilling it. He has no pleasure in fools; fulfill your vow. It is better not to vow than to make a vow and not fulfill it.*
> (Ecclesiastes 5:4–5)

While this passage relates to vows we make to God, I think it has application also to our daily lives. Some years ago, after reading this passage, I thought back on my vows. It was a sobering list: Marriage vow; oath as a member of the military; oath when I became a lawyer; and my promise of faithfulness as I joined my church. Memories came back of an early rural school room where I listened to a representative of the Women's Christian Temperance Union offer us youngsters the opportunity to "take the pledge" against alcohol. Time had dulled my memory and my sense of obligation after I had signed the promise. Reading this Biblical passage renewed it. The price of my vow was abstinence from alcohol.

Proverbs 20:25 warns:

> *It is a trap for a man to dedicate something rashly
> and only later to consider his vows.*

Perhaps my pledge had been made too rapidly and rashly, but Psalm 15:4 makes it clear that we are to keep our promises, once made, even when it works to our detriment. The Psalmist there clearly describes the person who dwells with God as one "who keeps his oath even when it hurts."

Of course there are exceptions, but in general, those who claim the name of Christ should be careful what we agree to do—and then to do it! If a follower of Jesus says it, others should be able to completely rely upon those statements. Such a lifestyle will honor God and attract others to Him, while reducing the likelihood of disputes and litigation.

This is not a new issue. The Prophet, Hosea, spoke of the same problem in ancient Israel as it headed toward national destruction, when he said:

> *They make many promises, take false oaths and make agreements;
> therefore lawsuits spring up like poisonous weeds
> in a plowed field.*
> (Hosea 10:4)

Therefore, we need to ask ourselves questions like these:

- "What promises are we making concerning promissory notes and mortgages?"

- "Are the tax returns and other government forms that we are filing under oath accurate and honoring to God, or will God and we be shamed if the truth were known?"
- "What other agreements, both verbal and written, are we making upon which others are relying?"

How sad for the follower of Jesus who breaks his promise and injures his credibility with others—and how sad for the cause of Christ when a believer violates his word while claiming to be Jesus's representative!

2. Should I Co-Sign?
The courts, including the bankruptcy courts, often have litigation involving co-signers, sureties, and guarantors. Proverbs cautions against this practice not once, but several times. For example:

My son, if you have put up security for your neighbor,
if you have struck hands in pledge for another,
if you have been trapped by what you said,
ensnared by the words of your mouth, then do this, my son, to free
yourself, since you have fallen into your neighbor's hands:
Go and humble yourself; press your plea with your neighbor!
Allow no sleep to your eyes, no slumber
to your eyelids. Free yourself like a gazelle
from the hand of the hunter,
like a bird from the snare of the fowler.
(Proverbs 6:1–5)

A man lacking in judgment strikes hands in pledge
and puts up security for his neighbor.
(Proverbs 17:18)

> *Do not be a man who strikes hands in pledge
> or puts up security for debts;
> if you lack the means to pay, your very bed
> will be snatched from under you.*
> (Proverbs 22:26–27)

If a co-signer is needed, it is doubtful if the loan should have been made to the principal borrower. Yet, co-signing is a common practice, particularly as a favor to relatives or friends. We need to understand that we may have to pay the debt at some future time. If that demand for payment comes at an inopportune time for us, litigation and possibly loss or even bankruptcy may be the result of our "favor." As noted above, the Bible wisely decries this practice. If others have needs, it may be our responsibility to give or to lend generously (Proverbs 22:9), but we do this out of *current* capital, not defer it to a later date, when we may be called upon to honor our promise at a time when we do not have money available.

So we should ask ourselves:

- "Where have I co-signed, and should I get released from these obligations?" and
- "What shall my answer be if I am asked in the future to co-sign as a 'favor' to friend, relative, or business associate?"

3. Should I "Leave Something on the Table"?

It is common practice for agreements to be hammered to the point that there is "nothing left on the table." Great pride is often taken in getting the last dime from a transaction.

The unfortunate fact is that this practice often contributes to the litigation load. Person after person can testify to problems that occurred because "we made too good a deal." Disputes often result when we buy, lease, or employ too cheaply or when we sell, rent or obtain employment at too high a price. Leviticus 23:22 says:

> *When you reap the harvest of your land, do not reap to the very edges of your field or gather the gleanings of your harvest. Leave them for the poor and the alien. I am the Lord your God.*

When we are fair and don't make exorbitant demands from either side of an agreement, it builds an opportunity for a successful relationship. It is not that we don't deal tough, nor at the market price. Such practices seldom seem to incur excessive litigation. But the *extraordinary* transactions where one side or the other, through ignorance or circumstances, agrees to terms that leave "nothing on the table" sets the stage for conflict. When the deal is too one-sided, the person on the wrong side may collapse under the weight or, when the opportunity arises, attempt to free himself (by litigation if necessary) from what he believes to be an unjust arrangement.

Obviously, those employed to negotiate for others have a responsibility to carry out the lawful and ethical position of those they represent. Thus, it is incumbent upon principals to set the tone of negotiations and the position they want to obtain rather than leaving this to the discretion of their negotiators.

So, we ask ourselves,

- "What "too good" agreements am I contemplating?
- "What agreements have I already made that need adjustment?"
- "Am I paying low wages to someone under financial stress who can't object—now?" or
- "Low rent to an unsophisticated or ailing landlord?" or
- "Buying with inside information of a pending change?"

4. What is my Responsibility for the Interests of Others?

This leads us to one of the most difficult problems in our highly competitive world: What is our responsibility for the interests of others? The first question man asked God was:

> *Am I my brother's keeper?*
> (Genesis 4:9)

We have been plagued with this issue ever since. Does God really say (and mean) that we have a responsibility for others—even our competitors and adversaries?

Jesus made it plain we are to love and to pray for even our enemies and not simply our "brothers." (Matthew 5:43–48) Paul stated the principle very clearly and succinctly in Philippians 2:3–4:

> *Do nothing out of selfish ambition or vain conceit, but in humility consider others better than yourselves.*
> *Each of you should look not only to your own interests, but also to the interests of others.*

Paul then used Jesus as a model of such humility in verses 5–8. God did not place us in this world to *beat* others (whether in religious, political, economic, or social environments), but to *serve* them (John 13:12–17; 2 Corinthians 4:5). While a competitive spirit is a valid emotion (like anger or fear), our real adversary is always evil and not other individuals. Our only real competitor is Satan (Ephesians 6:12). We are to fight against evil and Satan in order to save others, rather than fighting against others, while we serve and protect ourselves. This is not an easy issue in a hostile world. But if we follow biblical teachings and seek the best interests of others, we obviously lessen the chances of litigation.

Therefore, we need to ask ourselves continually,

"How will the position I am taking on this matter affect everyone involved?"

Years ago, a successful businessman gave me an invaluable insight as he helped me see that businesses have a responsibility not just to customers and owners—but to all those in the work community: the customers, the owner, the employees, the suppliers, and the community where we live. When we want more only for "me and mine," we may be sowing seeds of later litigation.

5. How Should I Hire?
Some time ago, I received a call from an acquaintance who had moved to another city. "I have been thinking of calling my former secretary and seeing if I could hire her to come and work

Vocation

for me here," he said. "Somehow I felt I should call and ask you first what you thought."

Out of my mouth, I heard these words, "Thou shalt not covet thy neighbor's maidservant nor his manservant." Frankly, I had never even thought of the issue before, but these words (which were a somewhat jumbled paraphrase of the Tenth Commandment found in Exodus 20:17) came tumbling out.

While it is common today to lure employees away from their jobs, it seems questionable that this meets Biblical principles. Why shouldn't we "steal" employees from others? The answer is simply that a trained employee is something (as well as someone) of value. If an employer spends time, energy, and money to train an employee only to have such employee "stolen," he loses something of value. The result of such transactions is often a lack of loyalty and responsibility between such employers and employees. Those who obtain employees through "headhunters" should not be surprised when they lose them the same way.

So we ask ourselves:

"How should we hire? On the open market, or by bold, but surreptitious calls to employees of competitors who have the skills (and sometimes the information) that we desire?"

Not only do the latter tactics provide a lessening of intrinsic loyalty, but trade secrets, customer lists, etc., are increasingly at risk. Litigation over issues under these circumstances is more likely to occur than within institutions in which employers and employees seek the common, long-term good rather than selfish, short-term advantage.

6. How Should I Advertise?

James, in chapter 3 of his biblical letter, points out some of the dangers of the tongue. The Book of Proverbs also has much to say about this subject. Several sections seem especially relevant to the world of advertising. For example, Proverbs 27:2 calls into question the whole emphasis on advertising, as it states:

> *Let another praise you, and not your own mouth;*
> *someone else, and not your own lips.*

However, assuming that advertising is appropriate in the modern world, other scriptures would seem to caution us about the *way* we advertise: For example, should we attack and downgrade our competitors (a practice that has become increasingly common in modern political and commercial advertising)? Proverbs 11:12 counsels:

> *A man who lacks judgment derides his neighbor,*
> *but a man of understanding holds his tongue.*

And what about "flattering" potential customers to get them to buy expensive items for "status" they don't possess? Proverbs 26:28 answers:

> *A lying tongue hates those it hurts,*
> *and a flattering mouth works ruin.*

And finally, what is the primary purpose of the advertising? The Bible says that Jesus "did not come to be served, but to serve" (Mark 10:45). As His ambassadors, shouldn't our goal be the same?

It has been said, "We earn a reputation; we buy advertising." We earn our reputation by service and performance. Legitimate advertising can enlarge our ability to serve. But advertising that promises but doesn't produce such service can result in disputes and litigation.

So we need to ask ourselves about each advertisement we give or receive,

> "Is the primary purpose to serve others, or to serve and build up the advertiser?"

7. What About Debt?

As a nation and as individuals, we have sunk deeply into debt. The writer of Proverbs, immediately after telling us to "train a child in the way he should go" (22:6), warns about the binding consequences of debt in verse 7:

> *The rich rule over the poor,*
> *and the borrower is servant to the lender.*

God understands there are times people need to borrow and to lend. He exhorts us to be generous (Matthew 5:42) and later quotes a parable in which the nonproductive steward was told:

> *Well, then, you should have put my money on deposit with the bankers, so that when I returned I would have received it back with interest.*
> (Matthew 25:27)

But God also provided a means of escaping debt so it did not bind people for life and sometimes for generations. Moses discussed the cancellation of debts each seven years in Deuteronomy 15. He notes that if we follow God's plan "there should be no poor among you," since those in the society with means would help those who were without. He notes, however, that there will always be poor people, thus evidencing that there will always be opportunity for us to give to keep our society in balance. Jesus echoed this position in Mark 14:7 as He says, *"The poor will always be among you"* and warns us to show compassion and mercy to those who are debtors. (See also Matthew 18:21–35.)

Modern bankruptcy laws are the legal machinery our nation uses to cancel debt. The biblical basis for these laws became evident when bankruptcy was made available only once each seven years. Bankruptcy is an overworked kind of litigation because debt is overworked. As we become awash in debt, we magnify the potential for bankruptcy litigation. Debt and bankruptcy have become so flagrant that we have now created a new specialty of lawyers who work primarily in the field of bankruptcy and corporation reorganization.

By contrast, the Bible urges us to live with a margin. (Proverbs 21:20; Matthew 25:1–13) As we told our children: "Always keep a little money in the bank and a little gas in the tank. It makes life so much easier." Unfortunately, those without a margin often find themselves with no alternative except to be involved in litigation in order to save themselves from total financial destruction.

Thus, we need to ask ourselves as individuals,

> "Should we eliminate some existing debt?" and
> "Should we not take on some new debt?"

And, as sellers or creditors,

> "Should we restrict credit to those who can probably repay rather than encouraging 'easy credit' to many who probably cannot?"

With individual, corporate, and government debt now reaching staggering proportions, we can obviously contribute to or lessen the chances of litigation by the manner in which we handle debt in our personal, corporate, and governmental lives.

8. How Should I Act Toward My Adversaries?
Many see those on the other side of the table as adversaries. This is particularly true in litigation, politics, and the field of collective bargaining between labor and management, where divisions often run deep and bitter.

The term "adversary" is defined by Webster as an "enemy." So we ask ourselves, "How do we treat such 'enemies'?"

Jesus gave us the answer:

> *You have heard that it was said, "Love your neighbor and hate your enemy." But I tell you: "Love your enemies and pray for those who persecute you, that you may be sons of your Father in heaven. He causes his sun to rise on the evil and the good, and sends rain on the righteous and the unrighteous. If you love those who love you, what reward will you get? Are not even the tax collectors doing that? And if you greet only your brothers, what are you doing more than others? Do not even pagans do that? Be perfect, therefore, as your heavenly Father is perfect."*
> (Matthew 5:43–48)

Paul, quoting in Romans 12:20 from the Book of Proverbs, shows this was not simply a New Testament statement uttered by a compassionate Jesus, but a theme that is rooted in the Old Testament and flows throughout the Bible.

It has been my personal experience, after years spent in collective bargaining negotiations, that it is not merely the "action," but also the "*re*-action," which controls the atmosphere in negotiations and working through solutions to problems. The principle is found in Proverbs 15:1:

> *A gentle answer turns away wrath,*
> *but a harsh word stirs up anger.*

Time and again, I find that a jabbing, sarcastic or bitter remark can be diffused when it is simply caught and laid aside rather than returned in kind. However, if our reaction is, "Oh, you want to play hardball," so we "burn one back," and the fight is on.

Again, in the short term, a "gentle answer" seems to be a losing proposition and totally out of step with modern negotiation techniques. Once we have been "put down" publicly, the natural tendency is to assert our power and authority in return. But this was not Jesus's way, as the Bible tells us:

> *When they hurled their insults at him, he did not retaliate; when he suffered, he made no threats. Instead, he entrusted himself to him who judges justly.*
> (1 Peter 2:23)

Therefore, we must always ask ourselves:

"Who am I trying to protect and to glorify?"

The real issue is whether our answer will lead to an escalation of the conflict in order to prove our power, or will we respond in a way that solves the problem rather than focusing on personal attacks and differences.

9 .How Fast Should I Resolve a Dispute?
Ecclesiastes says "there is a time for everything," and notes that God has made "everything beautiful in its time." (Ecclesiastes 3:1, 11)

The time for avoiding a dispute is *before* it happens. As Proverbs 17:14 says:

> *Starting a quarrel is like breaching a dam;*
> *so drop the matter before a dispute breaks out.*

Likewise, Proverbs 20:3:

> *It is to a man's honor to avoid strife,*
> *but every fool is quick to quarrel.*

Similarly, the time to settle a dispute that has already broken out is usually as quickly as possible. Jesus stated it this way:

> *Settle matters quickly with your adversary who is taking*
> *you to court. Do it while you are still with him on the way,*
> *or he may hand you over to the judge, and the judge may*
> *hand you over to the officer, and you may be thrown into*
> *prison. I tell you the truth, you will not get out*
> *until you have paid the last penny live at peace.*
> (Matthew 5:25–26)

Sometimes, we cannot avoid disputes and we simply have to wait until an appropriate time and circumstance to resolve the matter—either by trial through recognized authorities or when circumstances show the claim is without merit. Paul, writing in the Book of Romans, recognized that we might have this difficulty as he counseled:

> *If it is possible, as far as it depends on you,*
> *live at peace with everyone.*
> (Romans 12:18)

But we need to continually ask ourselves:

"Is there anyone with a smoldering dispute against us?"

If so, shouldn't we reconcile the dispute as quickly as possible so we can then be about our work?

This brings us to a final question we need to consider:

10. Should followers of Jesus Ever Use the Judicial System? As one who has attempted to apply God's law in an increasingly secular society, I have concluded this question actually has two parts:

A. Should believers sue one another in secular courts?
1 Corinthians 6:1–8 makes the issue clear:

> *If any of you has a dispute with another, dare he take it before the ungodly for judgment instead of before the saints? Do you not know that the saints will judge the world? And if you are to judge the world, are you not competent to judge trivial cases? Do you not know that we will judge angels? How much more the things of this life! Therefore, if you have disputes about such matters, appoint as judges even men of little account in the church! I say this to shame you. Is it possible that there is nobody among you wise enough to judge a dispute between believers? But instead, one brother goes to law against another— and this in front of unbelievers!*
> *The very fact that you have lawsuits among you means you have been completely defeated already. Why not rather be wronged? Why not rather be cheated? Instead, you yourselves cheat and do wrong, and you do this to your brothers.*

However, the church needs to provide the means for resolving such disputes among believers. Unfortunately, most church bodies do not have such a system or if they have a system, it is not being used. Alternatives are sometimes available through organizations, which provide mediators and arbitrators using Biblical principles to resolve disputes between brothers and sisters in Christ.

B. Should believers use secular judicial machinery when resolving disputes with nonbelievers?

Romans 13:1 states:

> *Everyone must submit himself to the governing authorities, for there is no authority except that which God has established. The authorities that exist have been established by God.*

As followers of Jesus, we are being used to help bring about the Kingdom of God. But in the meantime, we are subject, as far as conscience will allow, to the kingdoms within which we live. This would seem to include not only making laws through the legislative branch and implementing such laws through the executive branch, but also submitting to the judicial branch in order that disputes can be resolved.

Jesus allowed himself to be tried not only by church authorities but also by Pilate under the civil law (Matthew 26:57–67; 27:11–26). Paul went even further and utilized the secular law himself when he proclaimed, (Acts 25:11)

I appeal to Caesar!
(Acts 25:11)

Not to use church judicial machinery to resolve disputes among believers, or civil judicial machinery to resolve disputes between believers and nonbelievers, would seem to allow disputes to fester when they need to be resolved.

Conclusion

Those who follow Christ are called to be "the people of the Book," i.e., the Bible. We become distinctive as we listen to and obey God's word that He has preserved for us through the Scriptures. Often, this will cause us to speak and act contrary to our traditions and our peers. When this happens, we may be criticized or even shunned by others. Paul warns Timothy of this fact as he says:

> *In fact, everyone who wants to live a godly life in Christ Jesus will be persecuted...*
> (2 Timothy 3:12)

But it also causes us to speak and act in ways that are pleasing to God and ultimately to ourselves.

Great figures in the Bible often concluded that the need to follow God's word was a message of supreme importance that they must pass on to those who followed them. Listen to these statements given at critical times in the Bible:

Moses, to the Israelites as they concluded forty years of wandering in the desert:

> *This day I call heaven and earth as witnesses against you that I have set before you life and death, blessings and curses. Now choose life, so that you and your children may live...*
> (Deuteronomy 30:19)

Joshua, as the people prepared to invade the Promised Land:

> *Do not let this Book of the Law depart from your mouth; meditate on it day and night, so that you may be careful to do everything written in it. Then you will be prosperous and successful.*
> (Joshua 1:8)

Solomon, as he concluded a life of study, wealth, power and pleasure:

> *Now all has been heard; here is the conclusion of this matter: Fear God and keep his commandments, for this is the whole duty of man.*
> (Ecclesiastes 12:13)

Paul, as he "finished the race" and instructed young Timothy:

> *But as for you, continue in what you have learned and have become convinced of, because you know those from whom you learned it, and how from infancy you have known the holy Scriptures, which are able to make you wise for salvation through faith in Christ Jesus. All Scripture is God-breathed and is useful for teaching, rebuking, correcting and training in righteousness, so that the man of God may be thoroughly equipped for every good work.*
> (2 Timothy 3:14–17)

And *Jesus,* as He gave His last directives to the disciples shortly before his death:

Jesus replied, "If anyone loves me, he will obey my teaching. My Father will love him, and we will come to him and make our home with him. He who does not love me will not obey my teaching. These words you hear are not my own; they belong to the Father who sent me."
(John 14:23–24)

Perhaps many of us feel most strongly the need to pass on this message to future generations as we realize our own time is running short. As we grow older, we seem to empathize with the aging psalmist who entreated God:

Even when I am old and gray, do not forsake me, O God, till I declare your power to the next generation, your might to all who are to come.
(Psalm 71:18)

But Jesus made it clear in His final Great Commission that His followers are now responsible to make disciples of *all* nations, which includes "teaching them to obey *everything* I have commanded you," (emphasis supplied) (Matthew 28:20).

This is a lifelong task. It encompasses many subjects. But one subject, which seems of unique importance in our generation in this country, is to think, speak, and act so as to resolve (rather than to escalate) disputes and to avoid (rather than to encourage) litigation. Hopefully, the questions and Biblical discussions set forth above will help.

In the final analysis, it is not the words of this article, which are so important, but rather the realization that the Bible has the answers to these problems and to virtually all other problems if we will carefully study and obey God's directives to us. My hope is that all of us will seek to know and to apply Godly rather than earthly wisdom, keeping in mind that we all fail in certain areas and that we are saved only by God's grace.

However, that should not deter us from attempting to follow God's Biblical instruction to the best of our abilities. Several years ago, it was pointed out to me that the description of Godly wisdom given by James in Chapter 3, verse 17, is in fact a checklist that, if used, can help keep us on the road to peace. I believe that if we ask ourselves whether each of our contemplated thoughts, words, and actions are:

- *first of all pure;*
- *then peace loving,*
- *considerate,*
- *submissive,*
- *full of mercy and good fruit,*
- *impartial and sincere,*

we can have increasing confidence that we are becoming

peacemakers who sow in peace
in order to
raise a harvest of righteousness!

Part III
Harmony in the Work Place

Finally, all of you, live in harmony with one another....
(1 Peter 3:8a)

Preface

1978

I was fifty-three years old and had been writing professionally for many years. But one of my first major efforts to apply God's gifts and principles in the work world was to speak and write about the labor relation's arena where God had concentrated my law practice. I summarized it as follows in the chapter about Age 50–55 in Volume I *Four Generations*.

***

The Workplace
Most of my law practice was representing management in labor relation's matters, particularly those involving unions. For years, I had watched the battles of litigation, negotiations, and bitter, sometimes violent, strikes, which often left deep scars. It was hard not to become personally involved. At one point, we had our own office bombed.

Finally I decided there had to be a better way. For several months I analyzed twenty-five or thirty union disputes we had handled. Each night after work, I would sit in our basement reviewing these cases to determine, "What is causing such strife in the workplace?" I had thought that the issue would be about money. But as the cases gradually unfolded, I found that the issue was really about relationships; and that we usually fought about the money after the relationships were broken. I found there were four common problems and four scriptural antidotes:

Problem	Antidote
Faulty Supervision	Servant Leadership
Change	Co/mmunication
Incompetence	Discipline (As in Disciple)
Divided Houses	Security

As these principles were amplified, and then taught and applied by management, we began to see relationships strengthened and discord minimized. Never eliminated, since we are sinful people, but environments were changed for the better! I gradually began to see the validity of Dr. Trueblood's advice to me to return to my normal life, so that Jesus and His truths could be carried into my everyday surroundings and sphere of influence. Truth is truth. We don't have to quote chapter and verse in order to see it work.

The principles were presented in seminars and training sessions under the title, *Harmony in the Workplace*. Later, small booklets were prepared and sent to some of our clients and others I thought might have an interest. Again, the response was positive. I encourage you that God does provide ways for us to be used by Him in our workplace, if we rely upon Him and work in natural, rather than contrived ways. *And always for the benefit of those we are attempting to serve.*

***

It was fulfilling to see God move in the workplace. But it was also frustrating not to have the liberty to openly point others to Him as I presented His material. However, as I look back now, I have concluded there are always ways we can let Him use us. One of these is to be "salt" (Matthew 5: 13–16) and season the world around us wherever we are—remembering that if we "oversalt the beans, others may not eat them!"

It was gratifying, of course, to find that some heard His voice, as brought home to me by one seminar attendee who said with a smile, "I know where you get your stuff." I readily confessed!

As you read remember this was written over thirty years ago and much has changed in the workplace and in society. But people are the same. It is my prayer that making this material available again in this consolidated form will allow a new generation of readers to receive some insight into those earlier years and realize that God's principles and truths are applicable to every generation.

From Grandpa With Love

Section I

Leadership

Chapter 1

What's the Problem?—Faulty Supervision!

"What shall we do first, Marvin?" asked the older company president facing me across his desk. It was many years ago, and I was a young lawyer beginning to work in the area of labor relations. My client and I were discussing a crisis that I would watch repeated scores of times in the years to come. Tension ruled in his plant. Union agents were attempting to organize the plant workers and convince them to go union. Rumors were rampant. Written and verbal invectives were being hurled between opposing groups of employees, and between the management of the company and the union. The work force was torn, productivity was going down, and what had apparently been a peaceful, normal business, a few weeks before had become a hostile, foreboding battleground.

With all the exuberance of youth, I quickly outlined proposed solutions and courses of action. After patiently listening until I was finished, my older and wiser friend said,

"I don't think that's what we should do first.
 First, let's determine the problem!"

It has now been many years since that conference. During this time I have constantly come back to that question, "What is the problem?" I have concluded there are at least four basic problems, which cause disharmony in employer-employee relations in our modern American businesses: *Faulty Supervision, Change, Incompetence,* and *Divided Houses.* These four problems and their four corresponding solutions: *Leadership, Communication, Discipline,* and *Security,* comprise the subjects of this discussion.

In analyzing cases over the years, it has become increasingly clear that the foremost of these four problems is *Faulty Supervision.* Following are cases that illustrate various aspects of this most serious issue:

The Two-Headed Monster
The plant had been a recent acquisition from another company. In an effort to merge the old and the new operations, the former manager had been retained and a manager from the new owner's office in another area had been assigned as co-manager. The result was chaos. No one had final authority. Management slowly came to a halt.

Equal managers seem destined for failure because either could veto and nullify the action of the other. My own professional field is full of classic examples of this principle, as many young law partnerships die each year because there is no clear line of authority, no one to make the final decision.

Front Office Syndrome
Equally disastrous have been leaders who used their supervisory position for their own advantage and glory. Consider the newly purchased plant of several hundred workers whose labor relations had deteriorated badly over the past few years. The former management had spent great sums attempting to bridge the ever-widening

gap between the employees and the management. The personnel department had multiple lawyers and other staff with an annual budget of several hundred thousand dollars. High wages and the latest employee benefits, including totally paid medical insurance, pension programs, and other company-sponsored benefits, had all been granted in an unsuccessful effort to develop employee loyalty. Slick paper employee newspapers were prepared monthly, then bound into hardback volumes for perpetual retention. Despite all this activity, hundreds of written grievances had been filed each year and over thirty arbitration cases were "stockpiled" and unresolved.

Upon deeper investigation, one significant fact began to emerge: Management, including the personnel department, had not willingly spent time in the working area. Instead, they "managed" from a model office, separated geographically as well as emotionally from the employees. As a result, the employees felt that the first priority of the front office was its appearance from the outside.

Recently a friend laughingly recounted his conversation with a cemetery salesman who had called on him. Since my friend had been concerned about cost, he kept asking the salesman for cheaper ways to handle his burial. In desperation, the salesman had finally unveiled his best offer: "We will sell you a fiberglass box, which will then be enveloped in a magnificent bronze casket for the service. Then," said the salesman triumphantly, "when everyone leaves, we take away the casket for use by another person and bury you in the box!"

Front office employee relations are quite often like that—designed for show and appearance to outsiders. But all the employees inside get is a fiberglass box.

Wages and Benefits

Wages and benefits are not likely to be the principal factors that start a union campaign. However, after the breach occurs, wage and benefit comparisons often become extremely important campaign issues. And there are some cases, of course, in which compensation is so out of line with the norm that this problem in and of itself sends the employees out looking for a union to represent them. There are constant demands on any organization to satisfy employees, suppliers, customers, and stockholders. Each of these groups produces competing pressures for money. It is the responsibility of supervisors at the lower levels to work hard for fair compensation for their employees. Leaders at the higher levels must balance these wage requests with the positions of the stockholders, suppliers, and customers, who are also entitled to a fair share of the company dollar. Employer-employee relations naturally suffer when these management responsibilities are not properly performed.

Too Big or Too Little

Jobs, like clothing, must be the right size for the person involved. Often supervisors are placed in charge of part or all of an operation with the hope they will grow into the job as they are watched and corrected by their superiors. If the supervisor is close by so that his progress can be carefully monitored, the process often succeeds. However, significant problems occur when small supervisors are given big responsibilities and help is too far away. An example of this occurs when companies appoint branch division managers who are capable of being plant superintendents but do not have the unique personality and capability necessary to operate a total division. Time and again a union effort has been caused by a plant manager who was exported to direct a separate location but who did not have this entrepreneurial concept; therefore, he was not capable of understanding, communicating, and managing the complex intertwining of sales, manufacturing, finance, research and development, personnel, and other necessary elements of a total company operation.

Equally ineffective are supervisors who have outgrown their jobs and are not promoted. They frustrate and chafe until they move either up or out, or else they stagnate and begin to use their real talents and energies in antivocational activities. Use them or lose them!

Feelings or Facts
Emotional, temperamental, inconsistent erratics often draw followers to themselves, only to lose them. Cold, icy, impersonal logicians seldom have followers to lose. While such individuals may build and manage part or even all of a company, they also seem to be followed by a trail of relationship problems.

Cavalry chargers seem best equipped for short spurts but often wear out or drive out their subordinates over long distances. This style seems able to start but not to finish the whole race. Unless such an individual makes the transition by changing his style, or by turning responsibilities to stable long-distance runners while he seeks new challenges, the organization often falters and either dies or its originator is forced out in order that the company can survive.

Equally dangerous to long-range success are supervisors who have computer minds without accompanying feelings. Feared but not revered. Necessary to a company, but not whole enough to manage other employees.

Selfish Ambition—Bitter Jealousy
In an effort to determine what lay at the root of one union organizational effort, all the supervisors were brought together and asked, "What is the problem?"

Out poured the pent-up bitterness accumulated during past years! Like smoke from burned food, the manager's selfish ambition for his own success without regard to his subordinates had permeated into every area of the organization. Embittered themselves, the supervisors had effectively transmitted that bitterness to their own subordinates. In such cases, the prime concern of supervisors is often their own well-being. Because their superiors have abandoned them, they may seek to fend for themselves and make their own way, looking only to their own interests and not to the interests of their subordinates. Selfishness and jealousy are serious obstacles to successful management.

Sweet and Sour Spheres
As the National Labor Relations Board agent counted the votes, I heard the familiar, "yes, yes, yes, no, no, yes, no, no, no, yes." Notwithstanding the ballots had been shaken and mixed, the votes, as always, seemed grouped. Leaders tend to dominate the atmosphere around them: some are sweet and some are sour. If they are balanced, well-integrated, and carrying out an appropriate kind of supervision, the result is harmony among the people they supervise. Not without problems and not perfect, but a reasonable kind of harmony.

However, if a supervisor is chaotic and at war with himself, and/or others, he often produces that same chaos, warfare, and rebellion in the circle of employees around him. One such man seemed able to create so much dissension and strife in an organization that a union appeared not only desirable but also absolutely essential. He was once described as "the kind of man who can go into a room of smiling people and have them all mad at one another in thirteen minutes!"

If a supervisor is like that, the result can be employee rebellion.

Chapter 2
Lead By Serving

There are many definitions for a leader, but one very practical definition is: You must have followers. *If you look around and no one is following you—you are not a leader!* But, you ask, how can I accomplish this? How can I have employees follow me in the work world? The first answer is to *lead by serving.* A typical organizational chart of a single-unit business pictures the president at the top, and underneath are officers in charge of such departments as sales, finance, production, research, and personnel. Below each of these officers are then listed those who report to that person, and so on down the ladder, until we have a broad-based triangle with the president at the top and a foundation of rank-and-file employees holding up the entire organization.

Such a modern-day organizational chart is upside down for *leaders*, and the upside down thinking that produces such a chart has resulted in much of the conflict and warfare we experience between labor and management. In reality, *leaders* win their position by serving those they lead. Subordinates *voluntarily* accept such leadership because the leaders serve them. In these cases, the point of the organizational triangle is at the bottom, with the president supporting the organization through the tiers of managers and employees above him.

A supervisor is sometimes described as a person who commands his subordinates to do the necessary acts to help the supervisor succeed in reaching the supervisor's goals. Not true! That may be the description of an autocratic *commander*—but not of

Vocation

a *leader*. A leader is one who helps his subordinates successfully reach the portions of the total company goals they have the responsibility to achieve. As that happens, the leader in turn is then thrust forward and upward by his subordinates' successes.

I have recently watched a young child being served by his parents. In his earliest days, this little lad was bathed, dressed, fed, and rocked. All his needs were met by his parents with love and care fit for any young king. Yet he gave nothing visual in return. Only crying outbursts and messes, mixed with an occasional chortle, half-smile, or hint of recognition of the person holding him. I asked myself, "Why is it that this newest, weakest member of the family is served by the leaders?" And the answer was simply, "Because he is the weakest." So it is in all of life. Individuals are given various talents, strengths, and positions, including leadership, that they might serve others who need those gifts.

It has always awed me that Jesus, the greatest leader in history, would kneel and wash the feet of his followers! Yet, now I see it as an act of love for a weaker person, just as a parent bathes his weaker child. Leadership is not a gift to glorify the leader. Instead, like the gifts of beauty, intelligence, or wealth, it is to be used for the service of others, and someday the holder of each gift, including that of leadership, will be called to account.

Neither is it a gift to pervert to the leader's own selfish profit. Subordinates were not meant to be used nor abused by those given the gift of leadership. Obviously, all workers, including leaders, are entitled to receive fair compensation for their work. Leaders are necessary to help build companies. The question is:

What is the motive behind such building, and what is its effect on the others who participate in the enterprise? The problem comes if the leader uses his gift of leadership unduly for his own selfish ends, rather than also benefiting those who report to him. Much strife and industrial warfare comes from some leaders' use of the extra strength and ability they have been granted for their own profit. Such gifted leaders take this gift, that was meant to be for the benefit of the total organization, and squander it on themselves, building mammoth, profitable organizations, designed to provide principally for their own comfort and pleasure, while ignoring their responsibility to their subordinates.

But equally at fault are certain rebellious employees who refuse to carry out their responsibilities of obedience to those to whom they report. Instead, they claim their rights. They set themselves up in direct competition against their leaders. As a result, they do not earn the right to be led, and their actions often work to their own ultimate disadvantage. Unfortunately, such employees are sometimes spurred onward by governmental agencies, which encourage them to seek redress for alleged violations of new discrimination laws or by misguided union agents who deliberately fan the flames of discontent.

This was not meant to be. Each person was given the gift of leadership or the gift of service to benefit not only himself, but also the others in the total organization. These gifts were not given to allow one person to *compete* and wage war against his co-workers, but rather to *complete* the organization and make it whole. Only in this way can a company be the efficient, productive, and profitable organization it was meant to be.

There appear to be four basic institutions in our society: Family, Church, Government, and Business. In each of these institutions there is a leader and a follower relationship. The leaders have the responsibility to lead, and the followers have the responsibility to follow. When both carry out their roles properly, the individuals, as well as the corporate enterprise and those it serves, all prosper. However, when either the leader or follower role is abused or abandoned, the whole institution fails. Because the superiors are most gifted, they carry the heaviest responsibilities. They are to *act*, and the subordinates can then *react*. Thus, when the leaders lead, the followers can follow, but not until the leader first acts. And when the leader acts to serve his subordinates, they can react by serving him. It is the leaders' responsibility, therefore, to come in under their subordinates and serve them.

Interestingly, we have captured this concept of servant leaders in our political vocabulary in which we refer to our governmental leaders as public servants. Unfortunately, we tend to forget this concept in practice. The tremendous decline of respect for leadership and authority can often be traced directly to the failure of leaders to serve, and to the abuse of the gifts of leadership for the personal glory and gain of the leaders, coupled with the rebellious nature of followers, each who wants his own way!

Parents who seek their own fulfillment before they act to serve their family members must face the possibility of rebellious children. Church leaders, who seek prestige and power for themselves, rather than acting to serve their members, can expect the reaction of church splits and disintegration of the institutional church. Government leaders who act selfishly to seek power, prestige, and wealth from the trust, which has been granted to them in handling the lives and destiny of citizens (including billions of dollars of annual revenue), can expect citizens to react with contempt and rebellion. And finally, managers of businesses who *act* primarily for their own personal pleasure, prestige, power, or wealth can expect their employees to *react* by quitting, seeking union representation, or striking.

By contrast, those leaders who first act to serve their subordinates can expect a reaction of loyalty and service by their followers. In this way, the total organization can become a model of productivity and harmony as managers and employees all carry out the work established for them to do.

Chapter 3
The Key Is Caring

A group of about twenty men from various cities were seated in a circle discussing leadership. "I want each of you to think back to the person who has had the most important influence on your life," the leader said. "Do you have that person in mind?" They nodded. "All right," he said, "Now tell us, what was the most important fact about that person that caused this influence on you?"

The room was quiet for a moment. Then one man spoke one sentence, which was quickly echoed by many of the others:

> "He always had time for me."

To a leader, his followers are important people. Truly, he is like a shepherd with a flock, not driving them, but leading them and giving himself to them. When they are in difficulty, he cares. Thus, he does not see the appearance of an employee so much an interruption as an opportunity—an opportunity to carry out the work that he has been called to do as a leader.

It appears there are three basic types of workers: product-people; problem-people; and people-people. "Product-people" are thing or object oriented. They like to make a product, take it apart, use it, carry it, shine it, or own it. Usually they make their way into production work and their occupations, or at least their hobbies, find them working with their hands and using visible objects.

By contrast, "problem-people" are those who live in the world of the mind, working with abstract concepts and problems, arranging and rearranging complex situations, but sometimes unable to find their glasses perched on their forehead! These are people who often find their way into research and development, writing, or other creative jobs, trying to create a visible object, blueprint, or printed page, to express what earlier existed only in their minds. But neither of these kinds of people, without more, are leaders. Although they may be geniuses in producing goods or solving problems, they need another ingredient in order to lead. They must also have a hunger to work with people. They must be "people-people."

In an effort to determine who has this quality, you might ask this question: "When you see someone coming toward you, is your first thought to avoid that person in order to complete your own task, or do you have a desire to meet him before going on to your other work?" What about you, the reader? Are you willing to put down your own work to help a subordinate be successful in his? You must, you know, in order to be a leader.

Of course, we need to be both task-oriented and people-oriented. If we are totally dedicated to tasks, we become hard and calloused, using people to accomplish the tasks. Ironically, this is true even when the task may sometimes be to help other people; for example, a manager who uses his employees in order to help his customers. If, on the other hand, a manager is totally people-oriented, he becomes sentimental, soft, and unproductive. There must be a proper balance between the two. This balance occurs when a leader walks with his subordinates, accepting them in reality with their strengths and deficiencies, and allowing them to see at least some measure of his own at short-range.

There are many styles of leadership: some are volatile, some quiet; some are outgoing, some introverted; some are crude, some sophisticated. But all can have some success, despite substantial errors in methodology, if they care for their subordinates.

This principle was emphasized by a young lawyer who came into my office one day and said, "I've got it, and I know the answer!" "What do you know?" I asked, intrigued by the possibility of a new answer. "I know what the real issue is in a union organizational campaign," he said. "All right," I countered, "What is it?" He answered: "Who cares about me?"

As we discussed and analyzed, it became evident that his conclusion was true. Employees, like citizens in a political campaign, seldom understand the real issues about which they are to vote, whether those issues concern how best to run a business or a nation. We are not a democracy, but a republic. Consequently, we normally do not vote on the issues, but for the candidates we believe will best protect our own interest. As we choose our leaders, one of our prime questions is: "Who cares about me?" We are more willing to place our trust in a person if he truly cares about our well-being, and we do not believe he is going to use us for his own selfish interests.

To accomplish such caring leadership, managers must treat each employee as an individual. Collective bargaining makes that impossible, since the law requires decisions under such circumstances to be made on a collective, impersonal basis. By contrast, individual employment allows individual consideration, *but this personal relationship actually occurs only when leaders discipline themselves to take the necessary time, energy, and effort to interact with each of their employees as an individual!*

In practice, we are able to interact individually only with a very limited group of people. Jesus chose twelve to be "with Him." These were the followers who stayed with Him for a substantial period of time. Thousands walked with Him for a while, but ultimately, most of these "went away." Only the few stayed.

One owner of numerous businesses was asked, "How do you exercise control over such complex business operations as you have?" He replied, "I don't demand to personally supervise everything. How could I? We have ten thousand people on the direct payroll and 7,500 salesmen. I go on the old rule that you can supervise eight people well. You do that, and then you take one of those eight and have him supervise eight more under him."

While some individuals can supervise twelve, fifteen, or even more employees, the "rule of one to eight" is a good basic guideline for most supervisor-employee ratios. There is a temptation to economize by spreading supervision among fewer supervisors, which results in one individual being responsible for twenty-five to fifty others. Since one person normally cannot effectively lead this many individuals, informal subleaders come into action. These are magnet men, those to whom others are drawn. Sometimes they are recognized as lead men, gang leaders, or key personnel. But regardless of their formal title, their leadership is proven by the fact that other employees are attracted to them and follow them.

It is imperative, therefore, that such leaders be recognized and paid for this additional responsibility. Only in this way will they receive and recognize the kind of caring leadership from their superiors, which they need to pass on to those who follow them. Informal, unled leaders, when disappointed or ignored, often form the leadership for rebellion against formal leadership, which has failed adequately to recognize, train, and compensate them.

Chapter 4
Learn To Follow—Then Be A Model

A leader must also be a follower. A child learns to be a parent by walking through childhood with his parents, not by suddenly reaching puberty and being able to procreate. So it is with a leader—he does not become a leader simply by having the title of supervisor, manager, or even president bestowed upon him. Instead, the depth and maturity of his leadership is dependent upon how well he has walked and followed other leaders.

All of us are middlemen in the chain of authority. In the family, a parent looks up to his parent and down toward his children. At work, we also look both up and down the ladder of authority, and nothing so encourages an employee to follow his own leader as the realization that the leader is following the one above him. Ultimately, this requires that the chain extend to the model of our Heavenly Father and Master.

This principle of modeling is proving equally true in unions as they themselves grow and become businesses. One union business representative sitting across from me in negotiations was complaining about the struggle he and other paid representatives in his union were experiencing with their own leadership. "What you need is a good union to represent you," I chided him. Not grasping any humor in my remark, he answered, "Oh, we have that." He then pulled from his billfold a separate union card for union business representatives! Such irony should not surprise us. The foundation of much union representation is to resist company leadership and set up a counterforce within the company, not looking first to the best interests of the whole company, but rather, to the narrower self-interest of the represented group. It is little wonder then that the union philosophy spawns new unions to represent paid union representatives in conflict with their own leadership.

Loyalty and obedience are key words for any employee. They are the *quid pro quo,* the counterpart or consideration, for management's responsibility to lead and provide for the care and needs of the employees within the business structure. But they are not popular words today. On every hand, the public is being urged to renounce these archaic, old-fashioned terms.

It used to be that in preparing for a union election, employers were pleased to see the names of part-time student employees appear on the National Labor Relations Board election list, believing that these young people would naturally side with management and those in authority. Today, it is often reversed, as employers mentally throw the names of such students into the column of those they expect to vote for the union as the employer speculates on the outcome of a vote concerning union representation.

In addition, an even greater threat to the concept of company loyalty and obedience is arising within the ranks of management itself. Antidiscrimination employment laws originally sponsored to protect blacks in their work opportunities have now greatly expanded into a complex myriad of laws and regulations, restricting employers' action in many other areas of employee life, including religion, age, sex, and, physical and mental handicap. These laws and regulations cover not only hourly paid employees but also management itself. The result has been a rapidly growing incidence of disgruntled management (even including personnel directors and vice presidents), who receive information as privileged inside-management personnel and then file complaints against their companies claiming their employer has discriminated against them in violation of city, state, or federal laws. Both union representation and government antidiscrimination laws are secular methods devised to protect alleged rights and remedy alleged grievances.

If a company is to avoid such dissension within its own house, management needs to learn how to listen and solve employee grievances before they are taken outside. But management personnel also need to learn how to present their own grievances in a meaningful way to their leaders and patiently to work through these matters, rather than grumbling to their peers and subordinates or filing complaints with outside agencies or the news media.

Set forth below are some general thoughts for those who are in the middle, which includes most of us, since we usually play both roles, as we follow those in authority over us and lead those who are to follow us:

Honor the boss's position. Not because of his personality but because of his credentials. Respect for him will encourage respect from him.

Be obedient. People in authority are encouraged to do what is right, when they realize that subordinates are complying with the leader's directives (to the extent conscience and law allow) and much of the responsibility for success or failure is on him.

Be teachable. Listen carefully and be willing to change. It may be that we are wrong!

Be loyal. There is a place for rebellion but it is usually far beyond the place most of us are willing to go. Disloyalty and revolt is not the first action to be taken when we disagree, but the last.

Work wholeheartedly. There is a spirit of work as well as a form. Work done without heart, is discouraging, both to the worker and also to those around him, including his boss. But work done cheerfully and from the heart, is up-building and encouraging to the whole enterprise.

Take grievances about the boss to the boss. People very seldom work together without some degree of tension. Disagreements with those in authority over us are bound to occur, even when we act properly. But care should be taken not to discuss these problems with subordinates or peers until they are first taken to the person who can help. If our heart is right and our actions are right, our grievance will usually ultimately prevail. It may take time and patience, but in the process we will likely change not only our own boss, but also our peers and subordinates who are quietly watching to see how we handle our problems.

Managers are also models. Whether we like it or not, most of us are leading someone—at work, at home, or elsewhere. The question is not so much *whether* we are leading someone, but *where* and *how* are we leading them? What kind of example are we setting for them to follow? Do we really want them to become like us? Our subordinates often mirror us. If we don't like what we see in our subordinates (the mirrors), then we should change and they may change. Our natural inclination is to smash the mirror, i.e., get rid of the subordinate. But a better answer may be to allow ourselves to be changed for the better, and through us, others, including our subordinates, can be changed. This is a heavy responsibility.

Recently a friend related to me the following incident, which had made a profound impact on his life. He was sitting in his favorite den chair reading the evening newspaper. He sensed someone was in the room and looked up to see his fourteen-year old son carefully studying him. As he looked up, the boy asked him, "Dad, are you doing everything right?" (In an aside, my friend said to me, "That will make you lay your paper down!") Then he continued his story. "Well, I try to, son," he said. "Dad, you'd better be very careful," said the boy, "because I am watching you. I am going to walk in your exact footsteps."

And with that, the boy turned and walked out of the room!

This principle is equally true in business. For example, consider the case of a small business with about twenty employees. One day one of the new employees came to the owner and said, "This is a strange work place. I just realized that I am the only employee who smokes." A few days later, this same woman returned and said, "It really is a strange workplace. I have not heard any vile language used here." The owner concluded by saying, "I don't hire employees based upon whether they smoke or use foul language. I do hire the best people I can find for the job. But I am convinced the person at the top sets the example. The organization begins to reflect its management."

All this means that a leader must be in front. A person can *drive* from behind, but he cannot *lead* from that position. Being in front can be dangerous. In the military, it is called the point position—the first to take enemy fire. As a result, many leaders do not want to lead. Such reluctance has resulted in the enlisted men's tongue-in-cheek cliché, "Follow me, boys, I'm right behind you." But no one can lead from the rear. The leader must be visibly out in front, showing the way, if his people are to follow.

One of the healthiest single actions a leader in business can take is to walk through his company area daily. In addition, a leader must constantly review his own lifestyle and model what he wants his subordinates to become. Honesty, integrity, hard work, being teachable, and all the other attributes of good employees begin at the top. Subordinates watch and begin to duplicate their superiors.

One group of employees defended their own improprieties by pointing an accusing finger at certain supervisors, claiming "They had the scrap concession." Upon further inquiry, the employees explained that it had become common practice for these supervisors to designate usable material as scrap and then take it away for their own private use!

Leaders cannot say, "Don't do as I do, but do as I tell you to do." Employers cannot band together in trade organizations or mutual protection associations designed to collectivize against their suppliers or customers or employees without expecting their employees to band together into collective bargaining units of their own. We are what we do, not merely what we say. Leaders must say, do, and be that which they want their followers to become.

Managers must be good models!

Chapter 5

Don't Abdicate—Use Your Authority

"You can lead a horse to water, but you can't make him drink," is a well-known old saying. One leader's answer to that was, "You can if you salt the oats." Leaders need to become salt, which seasons the workplace and brings others to follow them.

But there is a time in our employment relationship when authority should be exercised. This can be true because there has not yet been time for a leader-follower relationship to be earned, or because a rebellious nature temporarily causes an employee to be obstinate or unteachable. Unfortunately, the term authority—like its counterpart, obedience—has also fallen on hard times. This concept is not in vogue in much of our society, which wants "to do our own thing." But it is a practical term and concept. There can be no organization, no security, and no well-being in any group without the use of authority to control those who cannot or will not voluntarily do what is right. In order that authority can be used more effectively in the work world, you may want to consider the following suggestions:

Grant supervisors actual authority
Titles without corresponding authority often fail. Some managers hesitate to delegate authority, either because they fear for their own security if a subordinate can do their job, or because they lack confidence in the subordinate they have selected. The size of a leader and the scope of his work will be determined by the quality and competence of the followers he attracts and

holds. Good leaders will not stay where they are not granted authority to act. Managers and organizations both need delegation of authority in order to grow.

Let both supervisors and employees know who is to exercise authority
In five of twelve local union campaigns recently reviewed, it was found that these efforts had either been started or openly aided by first-level supervisors. One supervisor seemed totally confused about his responsibility in the matter and said, "I was neutral. I invited the union agent and my employees to my basement so they could talk and decide among themselves what they wanted to do." What they decided was to follow the union leader. Obviously, if a supervisor doesn't understand his authority, or abdicates his leadership, his employees will turn to an outsider to fill the vacuum and provide the leadership they need.

Supervisors need to be willing to exercise their authority
This is hard for many supervisors. It may mean temporary unpopularity as justice and fairness are administered. But, however unpopular, the exercise of authority is sometimes necessary. There are always some who either cannot or will not work within the perimeters set by the company. A bad apple really can spoil the whole barrel—in a food market and in any other business.

Exercise of authority needs to be monitored
While some supervisors are hesitant to exercise their authority, others may abuse their power through hasty, angry, or ill-advised decisions. For them, "Power tends to corrupt, and absolute power

corrupts absolutely," as Lord Acton aptly stated. As a result, supervisors should be monitored to be sure they are properly exercising authority—neither too little nor too much; not driving, and not abdicating.

Conclusion

What, then, is the effect of real leadership? I believe it is the single, most important, factor to bring harmony and resulting productivity to the workplace. The Bible says it this way:

> *When one rules over men in righteousness,*
> *when he rules in the fear of God,*
> *he is like the light of morning at sunrise*
> *on a cloudless morning,*
> *like the brightness after rain*
> *that brings the grass from the earth"*
> 2 Samuel 23:3(b) & 4 (R.S.V.)

Such leadership is the sun and rain to the workplace, allowing it to bring forth the fruit it was meant to produce!

Section II

Communication

Chapter 1

What's the Problem?—Change!

I was sitting in an aisle seat on an airliner en route to a negotiation session. In preparation for a speech to be made a few days later on the subject of "Change," I was writing down various qualities associated with this word:

> **Change**
> Stimulating
> New
> Exciting
> Fear
> Discomfort
> Relearning
> Inevitable
> Necessary.

Across the aisle sat a middle-aged businessman. As the list expanded, he became more and more interested. Gradually he turned in his seat and leaned out across the aisle, the better to see each word as it appeared on the page. Finally he spoke: "Change!" he said. "I'll tell you a change I don't like. I don't like to fly!" (By this time we were at an altitude of about thirty thousand feet.) But he explained, "I found out what to do about it." As I looked at his tray table stacked with several small liquor bottles used by the airline for in-flight cocktails, I suspected what his solution might be. He continued, "I stop at the bar before the flight and have a few drinks. Then I have a few more cocktails on the flight. And do you know what?" he asked triumphantly. "By the time we arrive, I don't mind the change at all!" And sure enough, as he wove down the aisle after we landed, it was obvious he was well-insulated from the effects of any change.

Employees, too, are often upset by change. Fear of the unknown brings uneasiness, while the status quo is familiar and comfortable. Although the "old way" may not provide the best answers, nevertheless it is often preferred to other problems the employees imagine *might* result from change. This fear of change is one of the basic reasons the language of a union contract usually remains static over the years. Clauses, once negotiated, are tenaciously clung to, even though they throttle company flexibility and the long-range security of employees is threatened by failure of the company to remain competitive in the marketplace.

An example of this syndrome was the negotiation session I was flying to attend when I met my tipsy friend on the airline. The union contract of a recently acquired company had become virtually "fixed in concrete" over the preceding years. The agreement was bound in a small booklet encased in a yellow jacket and had become affectionately known as "The Yellow Book." Week after frustrating week, we pled, argued and cajoled for vital changes necessary for the company properly to operate its business. After thirteen sessions, the company still had not achieved one voluntary change—even the jacket of the booklet remained yellow! Not until the company endured a strike of over eight months was a new, more flexible, agreement finalized.

Desire for the status quo can also be seen in the area of union representation elections. Many efforts to bring in a union fail before enough strength is obtained to request the National Labor Relations Board to conduct an election. Even after unions get enough employee signatures to request an election, they usually win less than 50 percent of such elections. However, after a union does win an election and becomes the bargaining agent for a group of employees, that condition is unlikely to change. During the last reported year, there were 8,635 certification elections to determine if employees wanted to obtain a union, but only 849 *de*-certification elections to determine if they wanted to get rid of a union. The status quo is powerful!

Change (or fear of change) is another of the basic problems that must be faced and overcome in order to achieve harmonious employee relations. Such changes normally appear in at least three areas:

New Facilities. The glamour of new buildings rapidly fades when employees can't find the telephone, pencil sharpener, or tool bin. One near eruption occurred in a new hospital where the employees were angered because no coat racks had been ordered for their street coats. Not a very important item—unless it is *your* coat lying on the floor. It seems to calm the waters when employees are involved before all the decisions are finalized, e.g., the opportunity to make suggestions and discuss plans for the new facility; being updated with progress reports; and given orientation sessions, including "walk-throughs" prior to the actual change, so the new facility gradually becomes familiar, rather than having employees experience an abrupt, chaotic transfer with the employee relations shock it produces.

New Leadership. A second area of change is new leadership. An illustration of this came near the close of a meeting of divisional managers for a national company. One of the participants spoke: "Do you know our worst problem in this company? Our management now comes and goes so fast they don't have time to learn how we do things here before they move on to the next company and we get a new replacement. As a consequence, we have lost the unique management style that made us so successful in our earlier years."

Every company, like every individual, has a personality. As the company grows and personnel changes occur, so does the company's personality. That personality needs to evolve slowly like a stable, well-adjusted, gradually growing individual. Rapid turnover of management can produce a kind of industrial schizophrenia, which makes both the management and the employees unsure of who they really are—almost as if they want to ask, "Will the real XYZ Company supervision please stand up?"

There will, of course, be some changes in management. When this occurs, it is important that supervisors and employees spend time with one another at the *beginning* of their new relationship. A few sessions together can build a needed foundation to help the relationship survive. Such get-acquainted time is usually provided by the host at social gatherings. Companies should also provide this same courtesy to their employees. It is not a luxury but rather a necessity if a company desires good employee relations. Open communication of the new management's background and goals can cut through long periods of possible mistrust and suspicion. Failure to recognize the trauma of change in leadership has often caused open breaks in relations between employees and management.

New Procedures. Establishing a new timecard system, changing to a bank payroll plan, or instituting new rules and regulations have all sparked union campaigns. The new procedure may have had careful analysis by management before it was instituted, but it is strange and unsettling to employees when they first face this change. Cutbacks in overtime, or the possibility of layoffs or reduced work hours are even more serious. Changes such as these can strike unreasoned fear into the hearts of employees unable to cope with such financial catastrophes.

What, then, can be done about the problem of "change?" First, we must accept the fact that "change is here to stay." Edith Schaefer, in her book, *What Is a Family?* describes a family as a "mobile," similar to the ever changing decorations seen hanging from ceilings or trees, always in motion from wind or vibration. Businesses, also, are "mobiles;" always changing, and always in motion. Once we accept the inevitability of change, we must then learn to communicate when it occurs.

I believe a good rule is this: *"Only change as much as we can adequately communicate."* Obviously, gradual change is easier to absorb. However, great change can usually be handled adequately if it is accompanied by equally great communication. The more the change, the more the need to communicate. Unfortunately, change may cause management to be so busy it doesn't believe it has the time to spend in communicating to employees. The result is that there is often the least communication at the very time it is needed the most.

But change is vital and necessary to the continuation of the business life process. Therefore, it should be approached objectively; not shunning it as always disastrous, nor embracing it as always invigorating and exciting. Rather, testing carefully each proposed change, we should reject the bad and embrace the good. This can only be done through intelligent communication of the facts by the leaders, so the employees can become comfortable with this new change by being made aware of the same concepts, which caused management to react as it has chosen to do.

Remember, ignorance produces rumors, and rumors produce fear. By contrast, knowledge of the true facts, thorough careful communications, relieves this fear and gives employees the sense of security and assurance that their leaders are in control and that the change is one that can be used for the employees' benefit—or at least controlled so it will not destroy them.

Chapter 2

How We Ought to Speak

Clarity and simplicity in communication takes time and effort. Recently a manager was challenged to write a letter to his employees stating why they should vote against union representation in a forthcoming National Labor Relations Board election. "Put it on one page and make it so clear that it can be understood by a person with only a minimal education," he was instructed. A short time later, he returned and said, "I finally reduced my thoughts to one page. I was really proud of it when I gave it to my secretary, only to have her tell me she couldn't understand what I was saying!"

A few thoughts, which can be helpful in communicating, are as follows:

Watch Your Vocabulary
Large words are not necessarily the mark of knowledge. One couple's daughter suffered from a somewhat rare medical problem, which was diagnosed by a physician who thoroughly confused them with high-sounding medical terms. Sensing his inability to clearly define the problem, they sought the advice of an acknowledged specialist. After his examination, the specialist said, "The blood system is much like the plumbing system in a building." With a few simple diagrams and a short explanation, he explained the problem to them so they could make an intelligent decision. Whether or not a person really understands what he is saying is often revealed by whether or not he is able to explain it to someone else so they can understand it.

Use Bite-size Pieces

It has been said that we can eat even an elephant, if we use bite-size pieces. Communications must be broken into such pieces if we are not to be overwhelmed. As a friend admonished me one day, "Don't give me the whole loaf, just one slice at a time." A series of simple, single communications usually communicate better than one complicated masterpiece.

Say What You Mean

Watching witnesses review transcripts of their verbal testimony make it clear we often do not say what we mean. Seeing our words in print or hearing our voice over a tape recorder can have a most sobering effect as we exclaim, "Oh, no, I didn't mean it to sound like that!"

Start Where Your Listener Is

Leaders have the responsibility to accept employees where they are and help them move forward to where they should be. To do this, leaders need to see communications from the other person's vantage point. A simple example is the use of the word "strike." It can mean a labor dispute (which is bad), a missed baseball (which is bad or good, depending on whether you are the batter or the pitcher), a ten-pin bowling success (which is obviously good), or a trout snapping at your lure in a mountain stream (which, to a fisherman, is *very* good). What each word and each communication means to each of us depends on where we are when we hear it.

Watch Your Conduct

We communicate not only what we say, but also what we do. Conduct must be consistent with conversation. It is not "either/or" but "both/and." Both the conversation and the conduct of a leader must communicate clearly and simply the message he seeks to transmit to his employees.

Make the Most of the Time
We are stewards of time. Ultimately, it shows up in the profit or loss of a business, and of a life. If you were challenged to speak only three minutes to any person or group, what is the most important thing you would say to them in that time, and how would you say it to make your points most clearly understood? Many company conversations are brief but important. Organizing thoughts, then meeting faithfully in daily, weekly, monthly, quarterly, and yearly sessions, facilitates communication on a lasting and long-range basis.

Be Persuasive
Managers should accept this challenge: Speak to your employees in the same pleasant, persuasive tone, and attitude usually reserved for customers. Employees can no longer simply be "told," they also must be "sold." While there may be a legitimate time for deliberate anger with both customers and employees, its hasty use often blocks, rather than emphasizes, real communication.

If management will learn to apply the same salesmanship to *employee* relations as it does to *customer* relations, they can usually avoid serious breakdowns. The president of a small sales-oriented company stated two excellent rules for such salesmanship:

> "There are no successful arrogant salesmen."
> and
> "Salesmen can't be selfish with their time."

Vocation

Much good can come from companies training managers in some of the fundamental rules of salesmanship.

Praise and Admit
It helps when leaders learn to communicate to employees the employees' successes as well as their failures. Some supervisors seldom speak to their employees except to issue orders or to criticize the employee's performance. The employee's natural reaction, therefore, is one of fear and resentment each time the supervisor appears. Recently one company president was thanked by a customer for completing a rush job through extra effort and long overtime hours by some of the company's frontline employees. "Do me a favor," the president said to the customer. "Write me a letter thanking the people who made this happen." The customer willingly complied and the letter was passed on to the employees who received a real lift from this unexpected bit of praise and thanks for their additional effort.

It is difficult, of course, for supervisors to admit their own failures to their subordinates. However, much good can come from open admission of a "goof" by a leader to his employees. Willingness to accept blame, to admit error, and then to recover and go on to succeed can set an example that makes employees willing to adopt a similar healthy lifestyle.

"Salt" Your Conversation
There are words, which make us hungry and thirsty to hear more. These words draw us to the speaker. One mark of a leader seems to be his ability to coin and then use inviting language. These are the words, which "season" our communications and

make them convincing and attractive. Biblical language is such "salt." Note how often titles for books or movies are taken from scripture.

Answer the Question
Much communication is for the purpose of answering questions, which have or will arise. Once a question is asked (even subtly, or timidly, as in the case of a frightened employee), it should be answered quickly, completely, and accurately if management credibility is to be retained.

Speak the Truth
Never be devious. Never hide or shade a statement to an employee. If employees begin to believe a leader is not credible, they will not follow. This does not mean leaders should tell all they know to their subordinates. Many facts and discussions must be shielded from subordinates because they do not come within the employees' authority or responsibility and because it would be unfair to cause them to bear this burden. But what can be told should be explained with honesty and conviction.

Communication is similar to a good meal.

- First, comes the appetizer: a unique word or phrase at the beginning, which captures our imagination and gives us a hunger to hear more. Newspaper headlines, or the titles of books or chapters, are examples of this technique.
- Next, comes the main course. Not mixed-up "hash," but separate, solid, well-presented statements, which can clearly be understood.

- Finally, we bring out the dessert: something worth remembering, which will make us want to return again when a new communication is offered.

Managers must learn how properly to communicate if they are to feed their employees and help them to grow.

Chapter 3

Be Quick To Listen

Justice Douglas, speaking for the US Supreme Court on the desirability of grievance and arbitration procedures, said:

> "The processing of even **frivolous** claims
> may have therapeutic values
> of which those who are not a part of the plant environment
> may be quite unaware."
> (Steelworks v. Warrior & Gulf Nav. Co., 363 U.S. 564 (1960)).
> (Emphasis added).

This conclusion is contrary to the general rule of law, which holds that frivolous lawsuits are abhorred and should not clutter the courts. But the reason is obvious: *Those persons who are the subordinates in a closed economic institution need some way to be heard.* In the early days of new computer technology, college students had a saying for their frustration:

> "The only way to be heard
> is to bend your computer card!"

It is this same current of frustration that has brought public ombudsmen into governmental institutions, in an attempt to answer the growing cry, "Won't somebody hear me?"

Obviously, each person would like for his viewpoint to prevail. In court, much work and effort is used to persuade the judge to rule for "our side." But there is one thing often more precious than a favorable ruling, and that is our "day in court." Adverse rulings can usually be tolerated, but not adverse rulings without a hearing at which the litigants have an opportunity for their side of the case to be heard before a judgment is rendered. Employees, likewise, are usually willing to accept the decision of their leaders, even though adverse, if the employees have had an opportunity to be heard before final decisions are made on matters which directly affect them.

By nature, man seems to find it easier to talk than to listen. But following this natural inclination results in what one man called "one-way dicta," not *c*ommunication. *C*ommunication requires that information travel up the chain of command as well as down. To accomplish this, leaders must learn to listen. Aggressive, attentive listening is hard work. Yet there is nothing that compliments us more than an eager and expectant listener, especially if the listener is our leader who wants our comments before finalizing his own decisions.

While it is therapeutic to employees to be heard, it is equally important to leaders that they hear. Without such feedback, there is no way for leaders to tell whether their messages are getting through to their employees. One of the most common management complaints concerning communication with employees is: "We can communicate to the employees what *we* are thinking, if we will simply take the time and effort. But we can never seem to find out what *they* are thinking."

This was emphasized to me recently as a company personnel officer and I looked out at the stony, impassive faces of a group of supervisors thoroughly hardened to the prior management's presentations to them over the years. It was almost as if they now dared the new management to know their reactions. But by the end of the meeting, good, constructive, voluntary suggestions were being made by those supervisors, once they believed management was also listening to them and really wanted to hear what they had to say! Management must constantly lead, and then listen, to see whether or not they are being understood and followed. Then lead again. Such a "lead, listen, and lead" process needs to become a way of business life.

Leaders must be willing to listen to all the concerns of their followers if they wish full and complete *co*mmunication. Employees will not select for discussion only those matters that leaders believe are important. Years ago one supervisor was ridiculed as he held special meetings with his young workers to discuss "the pill." His answer was that this was a subject of concern to his employees and he needed to deal with it. The ridicule stopped when a union effort appeared and it became obvious this supervisor, unlike most others, quickly knew what was going on and had the loyalty of his portion of the work force because he had listened and then spoken to other needs.

Surprisingly, the matters that concern employees at their workplace are normally not particularly great in either size or number. More often than not, they relate to day-by-day concerns commonly known as "working conditions." Room temperatures, tool conditions, slight delays, are little things when viewed alone. Yet each problem is like a small rock in a shoe, which, when not removed, soon becomes the most important concern in life during a fourteen-mile hike.

Because many managers have not developed good listening abilities, professional listeners have appeared on the management scene. These are persons trained to listen and evaluate employee responses obtained through carefully detailed written "surveys" submitted to employees before any open difficulties arise. Through such formal communication, management attempts to break through the almost impenetrable shield of silence that so often prevents employees' thoughts and attitudes from reaching their supervisors. Another version of this professional listening procedure sometimes appears during the latter stage of employee relations difficulties, but before an actual union campaign begins. The technique for this is simple but effective:

Listen actively and openly, both individually and in groups.

- Take notes so the employees know they have been heard and their problems are being considered.
- Solve those problems that have a solution.
- Answer questions quickly and completely, even when it hurts.

Employees usually do not want to give up their bargaining rights to unions, and prefer to work directly with their own management once they believe they have been heard and considered, even though belatedly. If leaders are "quick to hear," they usually do not need to suffer through the pain and agony of this particular kind of employee brinkmanship.

Good listening involves using our eyes as well as our ears. Appellate courts are those courts that review the facts as presented in the testimony heard during the actual trial, together with the law as it applies to the case at issue, and make a decision whether to uphold or overrule the decision of the trial court. These appellate courts do not ordinarily judge the credibility of witnesses. Even though the appellate judges can read the transcript or even hear a transcription of witness testimony, they cannot *see* the witnesses as they speak. As a result, the law acknowledges that appellate judges are limited in their ability to judge the truthfulness of witnesses. The tone of the voice, the set of the face and shoulders, the directness of gaze, the shuffling of feet, and wringing of hands all communicate as loudly as words. If we are truly to listen, therefore, we must use our eyes as well as our ears.

Eyes can be used in many other ways to hear. Watch for clusters of employees who disband when a supervisor walks by. (If you are that supervisor, don't get too jumpy. They might be planning a surprise birthday party for you!) Watch also for other factors, which reflect discontent. One such signal is employee "turnover." Employees have only two ways to escape when no one hears them: quit or seek outside assistance. High turnover can indicate the company is not meeting employee needs. Written records of complaints are equally valuable to hear what employees are saying, especially when diagnosed for patterns that would begin to reflect a problem area or supervisor in the company.

Complaints need not always be verbal or written. Sometimes they are communicated by a "strained atmosphere." Such a strained atmosphere is emphatic by its silence and *lack* of verbalizing. It is the feeling you have when you go home to dinner and no one says there is any problem and yet you know someone is angry or hurt. The silence itself indicates there is a problem.

If you do not know whether or not you have any problems in employee relations, then you do have at least one: *co*mmunications. Employees do communicate their problems and frustrations to leaders who listen. Employee resignations and union organizational efforts do not happen unannounced. Some supervisors see employee relation's problems in their infancy and solve them. Others become aware only when there is open activity, such as the signing of union authorization cards or petitions. Once in a while, employers are totally deaf. They don't hear any discontent until picket signs carried by their irate employees appear at the front gate!

Employee *co*mmunications are like thermometers. They reflect the employee-relations health of a company. Unfortunately, some employers believe an ice bath, which silences complaints and gets rid of the high temperature, solves the problem. Not so. Silencing complaints in this way simply changes the common industrial cold to pneumonia—and that can be fatal!

Chapter 4
Avoid Hourglass Communications

In the hot summer plains country where we live, there is a shiny, black spider called the "black widow." She is identified by a bright red "hourglass" emblazoned on her underside, and she is deadly. Equally deadly are communications identified by this same "hourglass" pattern. *If all communications between management above and employees below are going only one way through one small opening, then that is "hourglass" communications!*

A classic illustration occurs when an outside union represents employees and most of the communications from the company pass through the union on their way to the employees. One small obstacle can plug up the opening and stop even these meager communications from flowing from the management to the employees.

But the problem needn't be that a union is the sole opening for communications. Management can create the same problem by dealing with selected representatives of employee committees, which they themselves have established for "efficiency." Or the problem can occur if the neck of the hourglass is controlled by a supervisor and there are no means of communication except through him. In each of these cases, communications are limited to that which the opening allows to pass.

People often ask, "What are the best means of communication?" The answer is: "There are no bad means of communications, are there? Isn't it like atomic energy? It can either light up a city or destroy it, depending upon whether we build a power plant or a bomb." Energy isn't good or bad, only the use we make of it. So it is with communications. The form of the communication is normally not good or bad. The real challenge is to communicate the proper information and to have enough communication devices so there is a free flow of such information, up and down, between management and its employees.

This requires that supervisors be bypassed, usually not by *instructions* and *directions*, since the chain of command is valid and necessary, but by various kinds of information that needs to be communicated in many ways. It also requires the long, hard, and tedious process of working between individuals rather than relying on the shorter, more efficient (but often less effective) means of mass communication with groups of employees.

However, after reviewing a myriad of the forms of communication that are available, we return to one simple fact: *daily face-to-face contact is the best*. How we speak, listen, and act each day is still our finest communication, and the best way to build relationships that can withstand the tensions and conflicts that can occur in every workplace.

Conclusion

Communications are the bridges we build to transmit thoughts, ideas, and feelings from one person to another. To be effective, these roadways must be repeatedly cleaned, repaired, and kept open. In addition, new means of communication must constantly be explored to get around obstacles, which seem to grow up in our paths.

One-way roads are not enough; communications must flow in both directions. One small opening is not enough; there must always be a multitude of ways through which managers and employees can bring their thoughts and ideas to one another. The leader's task in communications is to be sure that these roadways are always open and being used on a day-to-day basis. Only in this way can the problems caused by "change" be successfully overcome.

Section III

Discipline

Chapter 1

What's the Problem?—Incompetence!

We have moved from a "producer" to a "consumer" oriented society in my lifetime. For many years our courts protected producers by the rule *caveat emptor*—"Let the *buyer* beware." Today the opposite seems more nearly true. A rash of consumer legislation and governmental agencies, commingled with numerous court victories for plaintiffs in product liability cases make it clear that our public policy might now be stated *"caveat venditor"*—"Let the *seller* beware."

There are probably many complex reasons for this change, including the increasing distance between producer and consumer. However, one significant reason the rule has reversed is because we have become so intent upon using and consuming that we often do not spend sufficient time and effort to produce safe, quality goods and services! In short, many of us are more interested in eating the dinner than preparing it. So we pass laws and sue the cooks in an effort to make them do a better job. Ironically, "we" are both "cooks" and "consumers," so "we" are attempting to control "us." To paraphrase one comic strip philosopher: "We have met the enemy, and it is us."

The pathway we have traveled to produce this new public mood includes the following:

Division of Labor

Dividing labor tasks among many people as we do in the modern industrial society has had an explosive effect similar to the dividing of the atom. It has released untold energy for the cheaper and faster production of more goods and services, but it has caused substantial new problems with which we must cope. For example, it has allowed us to become efficient specialists; but this concentration on a small area of work often prevents the worker from seeing or comprehending the whole. Individuals become more productive more quickly as they repeat one labor function over and over again throughout the day; however, this repetitive monotony soon begins to threaten us as human beings, since we were designed to be creators, not merely assemblers who do not know the beginning nor the end of the product upon which we work. Obviously there are many complex economic and social factors involved in this problem. It is not my purpose nor within my expertise to define these. But acknowledging the effect of these factors upon relationships between employers and employees is critical if we are to bring harmony to our workplace.

Affluence

At the same time the workplace has become more frustrating and less fulfilling, it has also produced more goods and services from which to choose, and more compensation for employees. As a consequence, we are now financially able to try and satisfy our desire for meaning in life by indulging ourselves in pleasures and possessions that are being produced. The ability to produce more in less time through increasing technological advances, coupled with vast reservoirs of natural energy and raw materials, and spurred on by the growing numbers of individuals able to create and produce, have all had the effect of making available more goods and services than we "need." This abundance has naturally resulted in a cheapening and devaluation of material goods. We have entered the age of plastics, the era of the discard, and have become a throwaway society. For example, many clocks, appliances, and other items are no longer repaired—simply discarded and replaced. Obsolescence is sometimes planned, so we will buy for style and not durability. We frantically search for places to deposit our waste and abandoned goods and we clutter the land, the sea, and the atmosphere in the process. We have traded the fulfillment of creation for the thrill of consuming!

This syndrome now takes its toll in the workplace. Respect for tools and equipment, as well as the quest for quality in completed products, seems to decline year by year among employees. The vicious circle widens as individuals in their role as consumers demand ever-tightening controls against themselves as producers.

Governmental Intervention
If the workplace is unfulfilling but it produces additional compensation with less time and effort, it naturally motivates individuals to work less. This problem is then compounded by governmental action, which requires minimum wages for most work regardless of its economic value and protection for workers and their families during periods of nonwork, including unemployment compensation during economic layoffs, workman's compensation for lost work time due to industrial injuries, and social security compensation upon retirement, disability, or death. Finally, massive programs of governmental welfare overwhelm whole generations, distorting the motivation to be productive.

Absenteeism
All these factors have contributed to higher unemployment, absenteeism and tardiness. Many large companies now grant liberal vacation allowances of up to six weeks, paid holidays of up to eleven days, paid leave of absence for sickness, funeral, and jury service, and provide paid retirement as low as age fifty. Even so, absenteeism and tardiness have still become major problems in the modern workplace.

If work is not fulfilling and individuals are not required to work in order to survive, but rather are cared for at least minimally while not working, many will find their way "away." One friend dejectedly described his small business by saying, "It's not fun anymore." Upon inquiry, he outlined the problems of hiring and retaining employees not disciplined nor motivated to work. As an example, he related the following incident: "Yesterday," he said, "I finally had to fire one young man I had such high hopes for. He was a good worker except he just couldn't get to work on time. I even called him every morning in an effort to get him up and to work, but he just couldn't make it, so I finally had to let him go."

God knew that work was good for us. Since He was the creator and we were built in His image, we were also meant to create. However, He knew that we need an added incentive, so He gave us physical needs to assure our motivation to receive the benefits of the "recreating" we call "work." When we take away the fulfillment of creating and supply individuals with basic physical needs without working, we naturally encourage a mass exodus away from the workplace for many employees.

Overeducated but Undertrained
Over 50 percent of high-school graduates in our state enter college each year. Lured by a generation of advertising that

promised, "College graduates earn substantially more in a lifetime than noncollege graduates," and caught in the web of a social system that downgraded the value of "hand" work and elevated the social status of "head" work, we have produced many educated but untrained high-school and college graduates. These are "overeducated" individuals who become doubly bored with repetitive assembly work because they now need more mental activity both for challenge and for self-esteem. After struggling for years to obtain a "general" college education, they now find themselves ill-equipped for any specific area of work and spend their days moving boxes, fabricating products, or carrying out other manual jobs while their irritation and resentment smolders, waiting to break out into open warfare with their employers at the smallest provocation. There are, of course, many efforts to increase skills and craftsmanship through vo-tech schools and community colleges. In addition, there are efforts through universities and other organizations such as the American Management Association to train individuals to manage others. However, most companies have a severe need in this area, which needs to be faced.

Seniority vs. Merit
Standards of performance are increasingly being abandoned because of the difficulty of administering them and the pressure of employees to be treated equally without regard to merit or productivity. As a result, "seniority," i.e., length of service, often supplants capability as the criteria for advancement and continued employment. Congress, through its heavy use of seniority, has encouraged seniority as a *de facto* national policy, even though no actual legislation forces its use. While decisions based upon seniority may eliminate friction

caused by charges of favoritism, this system also discourages the advancement of the best employees and diminishes the motivation to excel.

Discrimination

The issue of "equality" brings us to one of the most serious problems in employer-employee relations today—discrimination laws and litigation. Following years of dominance of our society by white males, "antidiscrimination" court decisions and legislative statutes were set forth in the 1950s and 1960s. These were *negative* laws, designed to prevent further discrimination against persons because of such factors as race, sex, ancestry, or advanced age. The executive branch of government, in its zeal to remedy the effects of past discrimination, then began, by executive orders without vote or legislation, to issue massive *affirmative* orders designed to discriminate in favor of women and minorities as a class to balance the effect of past discrimination against them. It was almost as if the White-Male Team's turn "at bat" had come to an end. Now the Black, Brown, Red, Yellow, Physically, and Mentally Handicapped, Women's Team was to be preferred in hiring and advancement in order to bring about a statistical balance of handicapped and nonhandicapped, male and female, and all races, colors, and creeds, in every level of each business and governmental institution in our society. As a result, employers have become faced with liability, which staggers economic imagination and threatens the actual existence of various companies.

Public policy has decided that employers are the vehicle to remedy these past social injustices and companies are now required to implement and pay the cost of such *affirmative* action programs. Management's motivation to comply comes from fear of losing not only lawsuits with substantial money damages, (as well as possible payment of substantial fees for attorneys for both the company and their adversaries) but also the threat of being deprived of the benefit of governmental contracts. The result is that statistics concerning sex, age, race, and physical and mental handicaps of employees, like the statistics of earlier years as to seniority, are now an essential part of the business world. This reliance upon statistics further deteriorates merit and discourages employees' desire to excel. Recent "reverse discrimination" suits by qualified white males barred from jobs or graduate schools because of favoritism shown to disadvantaged minorities and females are the visible portion of a growing undercurrent of resentment and frustration, as people on *both* sides of these lines now complain, "I'm not going to be selected simply because of my race or sex or age."

In a bureaucratic society, we rely increasingly on form over substance. Counting years of service (seniority), or numbers of blacks or whites, and males or females (antidiscrimination), are "safe" means of determining who should be in the work force. By contrast, attempting to prove that one employee is more meritorious than another with less seniority or of a different sex, race, or age is subjective and fraught with the possibility of formal complaints and even litigation.

The result of all we have discussed in this chapter is that the "work ethic" with its emphasis on merit, excellence, and the need and desire to create, which dominated prior generations in this country, is declining in some areas. As a result, many employers now face a major problem—Incompetence.

Without debating the issues of whether or not the ills of our society justified the remedies, which have been imposed upon companies as a class, it becomes clear that individual employers are now doubly challenged to obtain and retain competent, productive employees. How leaders can be helped to accomplish this task in the face of the massive cultural and governmental obstacles facing them is set forth in the next two chapters.

Chapter 2

Choosing The Right Person

"Discipline" does not mean "punishment." It comes from the same root word as "disciple," which can be defined as a "learner" or "follower." Discipline means training.

Two elements are present in such discipling (discipline): First, choosing, and then, helping the followers to reach their full potential. At a dinner party one evening, a friend phrased it this way: "The XYZ Company does the best job of employee relations of any I know. They go to great lengths to choose the right person for each position—then they never let up on him!"

Jesus is the most famous discipler (disciplinarian). His first act in training the twelve men who were to walk closest with Him was to choose them carefully. The Bible records that He spent the night in prayer before making His selection. Much of the employment problems in today's workplace can be eliminated if modern leaders also choose their followers carefully. For example, production requirements brought on by unexpected sales can make *any* applicant appear worthwhile at the moment. Any choice becomes satisfactory, which will still the clamor for immediate help. Other factors, such as discrimination "goals" or "quotas" tempt employers to violate good hiring practices in an effort to bring their firm into the proper statistical balance of men and women, old and young, or black and white.

However, hiring applicants who are incompetent or unsuited for a job can have expensive consequences and pose a real dilemma for employers. If the applicant is hired and later terminated, there is the possibility of complaints or litigation by the employee, a union, or a governmental agency protesting the fairness of the company's decision. If, on the other hand, an incompetent employee is retained, this very incompetence endangers the productivity and morale of the entire work force.

One of the most important factors in choosing the right person is to look for those with a teachable spirit. Technical ability to perform a job is obviously important. However, individuals who are technically competent, but who come with an independent air, may never become a real part of the work family. Employees need to desire to fit in, if they are not to be constant irritants to the leader and to the rest of the team. One way to help determine whether an applicant is teachable, is for the hirer to ask himself this question: "Does the applicant come seeking and asking about rights and benefits, or does the applicant have a servant heart, seeking a place in which to serve?"

The company that my friend described at the dinner party as "going to great lengths to choose the right person for each position—then never letting up on him," has now hired hundreds of people over a period of years with very little turnover. An analysis of their practices reveals that each individual employee was carefully and patiently selected by a man gifted in choosing the right people. He built slowly but well. That manager has retired now, but he has left a legacy of capable, well-knit employees who have formed the foundation for a large, successful company.

Choosing the right employees is the first step in overcoming the problem of "incompetence." Only when this foundation has been laid can we begin to train a competent work team.

Chapter 3
Train—Don't Just Teach

Teaching is not training. We can teach thousands—as many as our messages can reach—but each of us will probably train only a few in a lifetime. The cost of "discipling" (training) is immense. It requires that we invest our life in another person, not to glorify ourselves, but to up-build and make the subordinate successful in the task assigned to him. Few of those in authority are willing to pay this price, even though this procedure will ultimately work to their benefit, also. Instead, we look for shortcuts.

Some companies bring in outside experts who give crash courses in management training. Although much *teaching* can take place in these situations, few of the managers are *trained*. Thus, when the teacher leaves, the students are often not strong enough alone to keep on in the new habit patterns and they return to the old, familiar courses of conduct. Other companies, not having invested the necessary years to train up their own leaders, "buy" individuals who are thought to have acquired such competence elsewhere and attempt to graft them into their management team. Again the results are second best. The trauma of change, unfamiliarity, and damage to morale of followers, who discover that promotions go to outsiders, shocks and permanently scars the organization. Although this method of trying to produce competence through outsiders is better than no method at all, it is inferior to discipling and training up strong, qualified employees and managers through the slow, tedious, and one-on-one process.

Vocation

There are at least four steps in such long-term discipline. If these steps are utilized, good habit patterns can be cultivated in place of bad ones, and many followers can be raised into mature, competent leaders capable of leading and training others.

Step 1 Teach

The first step in "discipling" (training) is to teach. A principal goal of teaching is to expose to the truth. It is to make the follower aware of the proper standard of conduct. If we are told, "It is snowing outside," and our gaze is directed through the window to the flakes that are falling, we intellectually comprehend this truth. However, we have not experienced snow as a fact in our life. We feel no cold, dampness, nor discomfort, nor are we now trained through experience to deal with the problems that snow can bring. But the truth that snow is falling must first be comprehended if we are later to become equipped to deal with the problems of snow.

In the workplace, this means that employees must clearly understand what is expected of them. This requires simple, well-expressed rules of procedure and conduct. It is usually helpful for the employees also to be told why such procedures are required in order that they may be better motivated to comply and ultimately pass this information on to those they are to train. The following principles may help those who want to be successful teachers:

> *Know your subject matter.* A teacher must clearly understand that which he wishes to teach to others. This requires that he be able to communicate the facts simply and understandably. Preparing to teach subordinates will crystallize facts and procedures in the teacher's own mind.

Communicating these facts and procedures will then strengthen and build up the confidence of both supervisor and subordinates in the supervisor's right to lead.

Experience the truth in your own life first. Teachers who speak only from learning and theory produce shallowness. Depth comes from experiencing truth in our own life. Leaders can best teach in areas in which they have first walked through the consequences of their words, so they can bring the full maturity of life into the principles they propose. This is one reason it is so important that the teaching and training of workers take place in the workplace by and through those who know it in practice as well as in theory.

Look for teachable moments. There are, in the lives of each of us, teachable moments—times when we are open and willing to learn. Why a teenager is a mysterious and closed person for days and then wants to talk and listen for advice at midnight after the parent has had a long hard day, I do not know. But it happens. Employees, too, are often receptive and willing to learn at times inconvenient to their leaders. But leaders will sense such occasions and sacrifice comfort and schedules to teach during these moments. When teaching must be arbitrarily scheduled, it is important that outside distractions be removed and the "learner" made as comfortable as possible, to achieve the best results. Thus, when possible, no telephone calls or other interruptions. Keep each session reasonable in length, with scheduled breaks. Provide good food at mealtimes, plus refreshments at intermissions. Learning is hard work. We all need all the help we can get to make it happen.

Step 2 Reprove

"Reproof" means to "see back," just as "return" means to reverse and "turn back." When we receive the "proof" from a photographic "negative," we see ourselves back through the camera's eye. Only through such a reproof or mirroring-back can we see our own face. We can go around the world, and, given enough time and energy, look into the faces of billions of people—but we will never see our own. The one face in the entire world we cannot see except through a photograph or mirror, is our own. As a result, each of us is normally unaware of how we appear to others. Watch as you or others go into a clothing store to buy a new outfit. As we stand before the full-length, three-portioned mirror, a look first of interest, then concern, and finally, incredulousness, crosses our face. We straighten our hair (if we have any), adjust our shirt or tie, or secretively wipe off our shoes as we see ourselves for the first time in full-length, living color as others have seen us all day! Until now we have been hidden from our own view. When we finally see ourselves as others see us, it can be a devastating experience, and we want to "break the mirror."

So it is with reproof concerning our lifestyles and habit patterns at work. When a supervisor mirrors back to us some of the hidden ugliness of what we say and do, we feel equally devastated. And we may mentally cry out, "Smash the supervisor (mirror)!" In fact, when reproof has not been properly handled, this has actually happened and an astonished supervisor has had to pick himself, and his glasses, up off the floor where both have landed! Therefore, in order that leaders and learners can best profit from reproof, the following cautions may be helpful:

Never reprove in public. It is bad enough suddenly to see my bumps and warts, without your revealing them publicly to peers. Habit surgery can be performed privately with some degree of success, but publicly shaming subordinates before others not only frustrates but also can embitter, employees and produce anger against a supervisor, which may never heal.

Never reprove in anger. Lashing out at a subordinate in anger does not up-build and change him. Instead, it can build an impenetrable shield around the heart, which prevents change. Since he cannot speak back, he may seethe inwardly and wait for a moment of revenge. Thus, rather than producing change, such angry reproof often produces retaliation at a later time against the supervisor—or the false tradition is carried on by the subordinate angrily lashing out at his subordinates.

Always reprove for their benefit, not yours. Discipline is first to make a subordinate, not ourselves, successful. Thus, when we reprove it is not to improve our appearance or position. We do not ask him to change "because you are bringing discredit on me," nor because "I intend to get that promotion and you aren't going to foul it up." Rather is because we want *him* to succeed. So we say something like this: "George, you have a particular habit that is keeping you from reaching your full potential. It is the habit of tardiness, but it can be changed. Will you work with me in this so you can succeed?"

Never needle or ridicule. Humor can be cruel. It is totally unfair to needle or ridicule a subordinate. He cannot fight back—only stand and suffer! Watch as an older child cleverly needles a younger one and then "innocently" looks on when the younger one finally explodes in tears and total frustration. Employees, too, have an explosion point. Leaders cannot afford the childish thrill of needling.

Remind them you also have a boss. We need to assure those who follow us that we, too, are undergoing reproof and change. Somehow it is easier to follow one who is also submitting to and under the authority of others. This is why the chain of command must extend, ultimately, to Heaven.

While reproof is difficult, it is necessary if we are to grow. Only by knowing where I err, can I change. "Teaching" gives us a standard for our actions. "Reproof" shows us where we have failed in relation to that standard. By teaching and reproof we are instructed through words. Then we are ready for action, to begin to work that truth into our life and to exchange bad habits for good ones.

In these last two steps we are now going to move from words to action as we apply "Correction" and then "Training."

Step 3 Correct

I sat in Chicago's O'Hare airport and watched discipline through action. A father had twice asked his two children to stop their bickering. As their volume gradually rose again for the third time, the father quietly stood up, took one child by each hand and seated one to his right and one to his left. Then he calmly sat down between them. The father had stopped instructing and started acting. He had *"corrected!"*

Words alone are not enough to change some conduct. Admonishing idlers and encouraging the faint-hearted may succeed. But in the areas in which we are weak we often need help. Dr Kenneth Cooper, author of *Aerobics* and other best-selling books, in a speech to about a thousand people at a recent leadership prayer breakfast, stated that the five most common causes of death for men in this country (heart attack, lung cancer, auto accident, sclerosis of the liver, and stroke) are largely preventable if we would use proper diet, exercise and seat belts, and abstain from liquor and tobacco. It is obvious we have been *taught* the truth about these evils. And we are usually *reproved* and know when we are under their control. Our problem is not *instruction*, it is *action*. How are we to overcome the evil and take it out of our lifestyle? Some make $500 bets they can't afford to lose—so they become either nonsmokers or covert hypocrites! Others go on crash diets, smoke weak cigarettes, or make New Year's resolutions; but, too often, such self-help courses fail. The key is that we are trying to *self*-discipline and few of us are able to win such battles.

A leader is one who supplies this missing discipline and takes the time to walk with another person like training wheels on a toddler's bike, until he can move straight and upright alone!

Step 4 Train
Years ago a friend of mine and I decided to enter the Army Air Corps (before it became known as the Air Force). Since my friend's father was a Colonel in the Air Corps, we asked him to give us one of the three necessary recommendations, which had to accompany our application. As we talked to the older officer about our new career, he reminisced, "Boys, let me tell you

about how I learned to fly. It was 1913. In those days, there was only room for one in the aircraft." (Perhaps you have seen one of those ancient airplanes in a photograph or museum: fragile wings and a pilot who looks as if he were sitting on nothing but wires and string, holding tightly onto a small control stick attached to the simple controls.) The colonel continued, "We had no paved runways; instead, we went out to the grass field where the plane was located. I got in and taxied up and down the field a few times. After a while, when I supposedly had gotten the 'hang of it', I was to 'Take her off.' That was the way I was 'trained' to fly!"

While some succeeded under this "training" method, I suspect the loss ratio was high!

By the time I learned to fly, the training technique had totally changed. I still recall the thrill of soloing, but it was preceded by a number of *dual f*lights in which an instructor had taken the time to fly with me and get me prepared to solo. This same dual instruction technique must be applied to the workplace, if many are to succeed. Unfortunately we often "train" managers or supervisors to "fly" in the same old way—we instruct them to "taxi up and down the field a few times" and then we hand them a group of employees and say, "Take her off!"

To disciple (train and discipline) followers, their leader must spend time with them. Only by walking together in a yoke of common endeavor, can followers be trained. These are key, costly words. That is why we train so few in our lifetime. It is a long, expensive process. But it is worth the effort since it eventually allows each person to multiply through his followers and frees him to go on to the higher work he was meant to accomplish. An older friend said it this way, "Remember, until you have trained a replacement, you are trapped—restricted to your present work. Training a subordinate doesn't threaten you; rather it frees you to go on."

As we have driven across the country on vacations with our youngsters, we have often broken the monotony counting the cars of trains as they pass by. On and on they come, always on the same track and always following the engine up ahead.

Employee training is like that. It also requires followers who follow along the same track, over and over again. Repetition is the final key to exchanging bad habits for good ones. We "train" to play a musical instrument, to fly an airplane, or to engage in a sport, through *repetitive* action. It isn't enough to be "taught" the standard, nor to be "reproved" so we know where we fail to measure up, nor even to be "corrected" and started in the right direction. We must also be "trained" by repeating the new action over and over again until it becomes a new habit. Each new venture is unsure and frightening. Yet, as we are disciplined over the months and years, we ultimately are able to solo and fly alone. And, finally, we are capable of instructing and training others!

Conclusion

"Discipline" is the principle we must employ if we are to replace "incompetence" with mature, competent followers, capable of working first alone and then "discipling" others. It is an ongoing process. Each generation in the workplace is responsible to raise up employees with the potential for competence and maturity and then patiently walk with them until this is achieved.

One reason "incompetence" has occurred on a massive scale is because we have been intent on consuming rather than creating, even in the area of skill and labor. The most exciting and fulfilling building process in the world is the building of people. Each of us must accept this challenge, rather than seeking and then consuming the competent individuals trained elsewhere by others, if the threat of "incompetence" is to be overcome.

Section IV

Security

Chapter 1

What's The Problem?—Divided Houses!

For the past quarter century, I have engaged in the practice of law. During these years, I have observed and been involved in conflict and turmoil, not only between strangers (such as those who met unfortunately but forcefully at some open intersection), but also between husband and wife, brother and sister, parent and child, and employer and employee. Lawsuits and negotiations involving divorce, child custody, business splits, unions and strikes have been the battlegrounds. Too often it has seemed the role of the lawyer has been to come into the courtroom after the relationship between two parties has been broken to argue and fight over the spoils: Who was to get the children? How were the acquisitions of a lifetime to be divided among heirs? How were the assets of a business to be divided upon sale or dissolution? What would be the terms of a collective bargain agreement, now that individual bargaining between the employer and each employee has been traded for union representation? As lawyers, we seemed often engaged in battling and "putting asunder" relationships that God had meant to continue harmoniously for good.

As the years progressed, my professional life became largely centered on management's role in employer-employee relations. I became more conscious each year of the terrible destruction and waste involved in the open, physical warfare of strikes, which sometimes included violence and intimidation, as well as the more contained but often deeply embittered disputes of labor negotiations, contract administration, and arbitration.

This all reached its climax for me one cold night in February 1964. The telephone shattered my sleep about 12:30 a.m., and my law partner opened the conversation abruptly with the unbelievable statement, "I just received a call from the police department. Our office has been bombed!" I had known of the possibility of such action, but somehow it had always seemed we "professionals" could stay apart from the seamier side of labor relations. When I arrived at the office a short time later, it was an appalling sight: windows broken, ceilings ripped apart, and doors blasted off their hinges. A simple, homemade concussion bomb, thrown through a window by two unknown men, had literally demolished our office. The next morning the newspapers again carried headlines similar to those which had become familiar to me over the years, but which now, for the first time, were very real and personal:

"Bomb Shatters Interior of Attorneys' Offices"

This headline spoke about *our* office! I had heard about industrial civil war and viewed its disastrous effects as a consultant, but now I understood it on a *personal* level!

Shortly before the Civil War over a hundred years ago, Abraham Lincoln proclaimed, "A house divided against itself cannot stand." This was not a new statement. It was earlier uttered nearly 2,000 years before by Jesus Christ, and that statement is true whether made in 30 A.D., 1858 A.D., 1964 A.D., or today—houses and nations divided *against themselves* will ultimately fall!

I have continued over the years to watch as picket lines erupt into mob violence, high powered rifles shoot into plants or homes, cars are ripped open and occupants beaten by normal peaceful and decent individuals who throw off individual conscience in the collective mob spirit, which all war, including industrial civil war, too often condones. All this has led me to the conclusion that more effort should be used to strengthen and try and heal relationships before they break apart, rather than simply fighting over the spoils after the break has occurred.

In order best to accomplish this goal of unity, we must first understand the ways in which our industrial houses are being divided. Later in this chapter, we can analyze some of the "second-best" methods, which have been employed in an effort to control the problem. Finally, in Chapter 2, *A Strong Man's House*, we will discuss what I believe are better ways in which strong leaders can begin to prevent split work families if such leaders are willing to spend the necessary time and effort.

Ways to Divide a Work Home

The most obvious division in the workplace is between "labor" and "management." The words themselves separate us. Terms such as "blue collar" and "white collar" immediately raise barriers between those who do or do not work primarily with their hands. Such divisions can cause envy by those looking "up" and arrogance by those looking "down." Sometimes this hostility is so intense it can be "felt" as you walk through a work place. In such cases, the atmosphere is tight, quiet, and devoid of any spirit of humor or openness.

Other group divisions can also be disruptive. Rivalries between departments such as "sales" and "production," with their conflicting pressures, can split a company into two competing camps and the civil war is on. "Jurisdictional disputes" can erupt at construction sites between competing trade union members. "This is *our* work," says one group. "We'll put a picket on the job and shut down the whole project unless the work is assigned to members of our craft."

Perhaps the worst split of all is that now being caused by the current "discrimination" craze that we spoke of earlier. It is pitting blacks against whites, women against men, old against young, and creed against creed, all who are claiming "equal" or even special rights for their particular group. While discrimination has obviously been practiced in the past *against* members of certain minority groups, it appears that a new era of discrimination *in favor* of minorities is now maturing under the guise of offsetting former discrimination!

A common ingredient of all these "movements" advocating black power, brown power, gray power, women power, or union power is that group members are banding together primarily to help themselves, rather than serving the company, the customers, or others not in their particular group!

The result is that we now see increasing evidence of a fracturing of our society with collective groups being pitted against other groups, each of which seeks special legislation and privileges to enhance the power and economic position of their particular members.

Second Best Solutions

Unions and other pressure groups are not the basic problems; rather, they are the result of such problems. One of the basic problems that has helped bring these power groups into existence is the failure of some leaders to properly protect and care for their followers. As a result, those in government have been persuaded to try and balance power between labor and management, blacks and whites, women and men, and old and young, by passing laws that will restrict the rights and privileges of the powerful ones and add weight to the "disadvantaged" group.

To accomplish this "balance of power," unions have been given additional rights, such as the right to strike, in an effort to gain concessions from management. In the area of discrimination, executive orders have forced "affirmative" discriminatory action in favor of women and minorities. In addition, "class" action claims may now be filed by one person for himself and all others of the "class" he claims have received discriminatory treatment—even though the others have made no claims of their own.

I believe such actions are second-best solutions to the problems. They are to the workplace as crutches would be to a person with a disabled leg. They may be better than no solution, but they are far less desirable than the free, agile movement, which would be possible if the broken member were healed. It is hoped, of course, by those who advocate such laws, that healing will take place during the period of restricted activity and that the crutches (laws) can ultimately be removed. In practice, the opposite seems to have happened. Laws are not usually removed, only added. As a result, we are increasingly in danger of becoming permanently handicapped as we rely more and more on outside crutches provided by government to solve our problems.

In addition, government itself is now being stricken with the same illnesses it set out to control and cure in the private business world. For example, let's look at the area of "collective bargaining." In 1935 Congress passed the National Labor Relations Act, which required employers to recognize and bargain collectively with unions that properly represented a group of employees. The result was that millions of private employees entered the union ranks during the next few years.

As this occurred, governmental employees quite logically asked, "If collective bargaining rights are valid to restrict the power of private employers, why not impose these same restrictions on government, which is now the largest and fastest-growing, all-powerful employer in the nation?" And so it has happened. Starting with legislation adopted by Wisconsin in 1959, there began a rush toward unionization of governmental employees. Today, while industrial unions are losing members, public employee unions are gaining members. Although public employees are usually denied the right to strike, governments sometimes find themselves threatened with paralysis of their fire departments, schools, collection of refuse, and police and sheriff departments through "sick days" or other thinly veiled strike tactics.

Our businesses and our governments (like our families and our churches) are meant to operate in harmony—not in division and discord. This is accomplished when each person does their work not only for their own benefit, but also for the benefit of the others involved in the enterprise. By contrast, our collective bargaining laws (in an effort to control those who have failed to control themselves) now encourage us to be divided within our work places into opposing power blocks of labor and management. And our antidiscrimination laws increasingly divide us into hopelessly scrambled statistical groups based on sex, race, religion, age, physical, and mental handicap and national origin.

Let me emphasize again that unions and other power groups are not the problem, rather they result from the problem; and sometimes, like divorce or revolution, they seem to be the only alternative after a situation has deteriorated to an intolerable condition.

But divorce, revolution, unions, and peer power blocs are "second-best" solutions to the problem. The best solution is for leaders properly to conduct themselves so that their houses will not divide! The next chapter discusses a style of leadership designed to help retain such unity.

Chapter 2
A Strong Man's House

"Unions are for the weak!" said the attorney for a large union as we spoke philosophically about the labor movement in the United States. He continued, "Those of us who are unable to succeed in a competitive society join unions to survive." At first, I felt a surge of superiority as I heard this confession; but as I have reflected on his statement over many years, I have concluded, "*All* of us are weak!" *All* of us in the work world need one another to survive—from presidents to janitors, and from mayors to garbage collectors. If anyone does not realize this interdependence, let the trash and waste accumulate for six weeks and see how well we function! The answer for all of us is to unite for strength—the problem is not *whether* to unite, but *what is the proper group form* for such unity?

As we discussed in the last chapter, peer groups (such as unions or minorities) are "second-best" forms, since these often sow the seeds of company division and destruction. Instead, the work institution itself should be the form into which we unite for strength in the work world. This requires strong leaders with appropriate talents and abilities who are dedicated to benefiting the entire organization, not merely themselves or their management team.

Despite popular misconceptions to the contrary, these leaders are seldom, if ever, "self-made" men. Rather, they are principally the beneficiaries of a combination of gifts. First is their gift of unique mental and/or physical ability. These inherited traits are often accompanied by gifts of training by inspired parents, teachers, or others who have poured their lives into making these leaders strong and successful. These gifts are then honed and made usable by the individual commitment and personal effort of each leader. Such leaders have tremendous responsibilities. They must now pour the strength of these gifts into their followers. They cannot abdicate their function or the company will become weak and fail in the competitive marketplace. Neither can they use their strength to abuse their followers for their own undue profit and glorification. If this happens, these employees will seek someone stronger (such as a union or governmental agency) to bind the employer so it can no longer injure them. An example of this reaction was contained in an anonymous letter from a group of minimum wage employees to the president during a union organizing effort. The letter read, in part:

> You may know that most of us signed to go union, which should come to a vote soon. But this wasn't done for the money as much as for job security.

"Security!" This is to followers, what "opportunity" is to leaders. This need can exist not only in lower echelon employees, but also up into the ranks of management. This was revealed graphically during discussion with a group of middle managers who had come together for a week of management training at a state university. One finally confessed, "You get to the point where you believe the only safe place is on the board of directors or in the union!"

Good leaders are careful to provide the atmosphere and actions, which will ensure this sense of security for their subordinates who have placed themselves under the leaders' care and protection. Several elements should be considered in providing this *real job security*, which makes union organization or governmental intervention an undesirable alternative for followers in a strong business structure. Listed below are some examples:

A Steady Job
Job security in its rawest form means a job itself with little likelihood of layoff or shutdown. Unions flourish in fluctuating, unstable industries. Construction work has long been union dominated. One reason is because employment conditions are unstable. Hiring is often dependent upon the union hiring hall rather than upon any single employer. As a result, construction employees may come to look upon a union rather than a company as their actual employer. One young woman verbalized this in answer to the question, "What does your father do?" by responding, "Oh, he works for the union. He's a carpenter."

Stable, year-round employment even at lower pay, is often more logical and attractive than higher pay accompanied by frequent layoffs and the uncertainty it causes. Nonunion construction companies adopting this philosophy are growing rapidly. "Up and down" employment sends employees to unions or to the government for security, which the employer has failed to provide. Frequent layoffs by some companies have encouraged expensive unemployment taxes against all employers. Hiring for the short term with consequent layoffs has brought on union organizational efforts by insecure employees. On balance, some companies find it is better to forego the short-term profit from short-term hiring and be content with slower, but stronger, permanent growth.

Fair Pay
Once a job has been obtained, the next question is pay. A person who truly leads, strives to make his followers successful. This includes helping them increase their earnings. A man recently said he left the employ of a certain company. When asked, "Why?" he answered, "They'll never let you make any money. As a result, they have never been able to keep anyone for a long period of time."

By contrast, another company has been particularly impressive in the area of increasing employee wages. They are producing today ten times as much product as they were a few years ago, but with the same number of employees. The key has been a willingness by management to invest large sums in automated equipment. This in turn keeps the company ahead of its competition in both quality and quantity, thereby allowing the employees to make far higher wages than their union counterparts, as these nonunion workers accept the responsibility to be retrained to handle this new equipment and to be motivated by strict standards of accountability. When a union recently sent in out-of-town organizers to unionize this company, management held small group meetings and went through the current contract in force between a competitor and the organizing union. Item by item, clause by clause, they showed the employees in "black and white" how much better the nonunion operation had been able to compensate its employees. When the vote arrived, it was over five to one against the union!

Leaders are said to have the ability to see further in advance than their followers. It is as if they somehow know what lies ahead and around the next corner. Whether this occurs because of past experience, or by some internal calculator that adds together the known facts and comes up with the correct (though previously unknown) answer, it is a key ingredient of leadership. We desire to follow those who seem to know where they are going and how to get there.

Management has the obligation to study carefully and then formulate the goals and policies of the company for the mutual benefit of the employees, the management, the stockholders, and those with whom it does business; to finance these goals and policies; and to provide leadership to carry out these goals and policies. As a part of such self-disciplined leadership, employers should pay more, not less, because their company is nonunion. More wages should be available because of the vast freedom and opportunity the company has to be flexible and build in efficiency, while weeding out mediocrity and featherbedding.

Additional Job Benefits
After a stable job is obtained with fair pay, there seems to be an ascending order in the financial desires of employees. The steps often fade in our minds as they are achieved. Yesterday's desires, once obtained, often become today's necessities. The following appear to be the order of many employees' financial desires as they develop:

- A stable job
- Fair pay
- Protection against immediate disaster (medical insurance)
- Time off (break periods, holidays, vacation)
- Protection for the future (pension, life insurance, disability insurance)
- The opportunity to become a capitalist (savings plans, stock purchase plans, profit sharing)

If these desires are reasonably provided by the company, in general accord with industry and area practices, then employees loyalty will likely be with the company—rather than with outsiders who do not contribute to the productive activity of the employees, but, instead, live off of these employees through dues or taxes as the price for the security they claim they can provide to the employees.

Strong Enough to Trust
There is another rather subtle kind of protection, which leaders also need to provide for their followers. It requires applying strength fairly but firmly to correct and control the *good* employees who occasionally rebel in an almost unconscious test of their leader's strength. If the leader can overcome such rebellion, his strength assures the employees that they and the organization are secure. If the leader is unable to withstand such internal attacks, he obviously is too impotent to be trustworthy, and the house becomes divided with all the attendant consequences. One employee phrased it this way:

> "Persons who are employed realize they must have a job to support whatever is their lifestyle. Therefore, they are strong enough to want to work, but this same strength causes them to rebel occasionally in order to test just how strong is the person over them. If they find that person is still stronger than they are, they will respect him. If they find that person is *not* stronger, they will not do what he tells them."

Exercising sufficient control to overcome such minor uprisings also brings a sense of security to the other noninvolved employees. Nothing deteriorates an organization more quickly than failure to control the "rebels" while forcing the "meek" to comply. By contrast, nothing gives a greater sense of security than observing leaders strong enough to deal fairly and decisively with attacks either from inside or outside the organization.

The Total Quality of Life
There is at least one more responsibility that management should consider if it is to avoid a divided house. It involves helping each employee be an integrated, undivided person. This in turn requires leaders to provide a workplace that will contribute toward the total quality of life for each employee. Following are some suggestions that may help accomplish this:

> *Creative Work.* Leaders should provide good work in an atmosphere designed to be fulfilling to the employees. Since God created us in His image, we, too, are creators. We have an inborn desire to work. One of life's greatest pearls is doing the kind of work we desire, with people with whom we desire to do it. One of the great challenges of a leader is to create a workplace that will allow the employees also to create and thereby be fulfilled.

> *A Spiritual Base.* Leaders should also protect the spiritual life of their employees. Voluntary protection of spiritual needs will draw followers to leaders and to the spiritual values that cause the leaders to protect their subordinates' spiritual health. Expression of a leader's creed is one important component of leadership. One successful businessman with whom I have been well-acquainted has the following plaque on his wall:

*"The purpose of (name of company) is to operate a
(type of business—food store, law office, etc.)
to the glory of God."*

Such public expressions may be met with criticism. Fear of criticism often silences. However, leaders have the responsibility to lead and speak out because they are leading. Without a voice and a direction, employees do not know which way to go. Such boldness, combined with protection of the spiritual climate of subordinates, can help produce healthy, growing employees. As an additional effort, some businesses are today providing industrial chaplains. These men are being hired not to convert all the employees to their particular faith, but to bring a visible spiritual emphasis to the workplace, and to give spiritual support to an employee whose personal world is breaking apart and threatening to destroy him as a person.

Economic and Physical Health. In a nation enjoying unparalleled material prosperity, we continue to have many with poor economic and physical health. Easy credit offered enticingly to purchasers, attractive ads featuring smiling lenders—coupled with a government policy of ever-increasing public debt and planned inflation by increasing the money supply, which encourages us to borrow now and pay back in later years with cheaper dollars, have plunged many into the "debt trap." In like manner, the "good life," with its rich food, intoxicating drinks, and easy living, has deteriorated the physical health of many. To counteract these twin perils some employers have begun education programs designed to acquaint employees with these problems and possible solutions. Since employees who cannot manage their money well are often in financial difficulties, which affect their work performance as well as their private lives, it only makes economic sense to instruct them in how they can help avoid the problems of excessive debt and the nightmares it can cause. In like manner, some companies not only supply health insurance for treating illness after it occurs, but also provide education to prevent illness before it begins. Monthly health letters, seminars, and bulletins by cooperating insurance companies, together with annual checkups and exercise programs, all help to maintain a healthier, more efficient work force, thereby aiding the individual employees and the total work organization.

Family Life

One scourge and curse of America today is the deterioration of the family unit. The last generation's massive tandem marriages interrupted by multiple divorces, has now descended into this generation's casual living arrangements often without benefit of marriage. By example of leaders and by education of employees, it can be shown as well as taught that there is a better lifestyle available through the traditional family structure. Leadership in this area requires exemplary living by the leaders and being careful that temptations are not placed in the path of those subordinates who cannot withstand them. It requires subtle encouragement, including sufficient time off to maintain good family life, and encouragement for followers to put their lives in proper perspective—God first, family second, and work third. A high percentage of the divorces I have witnessed are caused or encouraged because a spouse places work first above the other spouse and family.

Years ago, I believed the cliché, "The customer comes first, above home, employees or other priorities." When I announced this to my partners, it was met with stony silence. While it helped build my business during the early years, it ultimately caused problems. Now I realize we need first to protect our home, then our own office team—in effect, build solidly from the inside out, if we want to become strong enough to give customers the long-term help to which they are entitled.

Institutions do not falter and die separately. As the family structures fail in our society, there is a corresponding failure of our other institutions, including the workplace. Only by encouraging employees, and helping them to live properly in *all* areas of their lives, can the institution we know as "business" be most efficient and fulfilling.

Conclusion

The antidote to a divided house is strong leadership, which uses its strength to protect its followers from internal and external attacks. It is competitive, efficient, and tough in the marketplaces of the world. It does not ask for economic help from government or peers, because it knows the price will ultimately be to bind it. It fights any effort by those who would divide the working home against itself. But it will never, never use its strength for undue gain or greedy advantage of its weaker employees—since leaders will ultimately be called to account for the way in which they have handled the gifts of strength and capability bestowed upon them.

Reflections

2007

It has been a nostalgic and rather startling exercise for me to look back over 50 years and revisit this material from experiences that began in the mid-1950s, that I placed in writing in 1978, and then continued to use until my retirement from the practice of law at the close of 1994.

I am deeply indebted to all my partners and others with whom I worked over the years, for granting me the freedom to carry out the work that I felt God was calling me to do during this part of my life—and to my wife and family for enduring through all the learning that needed to occur before I was fully aware that God was calling us all to "Harmony in the Workplace," rather than the conflict, which so often happens.

I now realize that the principles I learned in those earlier years in the workplace are equally applicable to the other three institutions of the Family, Church, and Government. How I yearn to see leaders and followers in every group use Biblical principles, which call us all to *"complete—not compete"* with others.

It is as if God wants to conduct a wondrous human orchestra, designed to make beautiful music as He fits each unique note in with all the other notes in a "Heavenly Harmony" for our enjoyment and His Glory. We only have to obey!

From Grandpa With Love!

Part IV
Working With Words

*If anyone speaks, he should do it as one speaking
the very words of God...so that in all things
God may be praised through Jesus Christ.
To Him be the glory and the power for ever and ever.
Amen.*
(1 Peter 4:11)

Working With Words

Communication is one of God's great gifts. It comes from the same root word as "community" or "communion." Its purpose is to bring us together.

We communicate by both "words" and "works." We need both. There are a few people who use both equally well. Most of us major in one or the other.

I am primarily a "word worker." For over fifty years, first as a lawyer and later in teaching and writing, it has been my task to communicate with words. To question, to explain, to persuade, but always using words.

Let me give you a few thoughts about what I have learned and tried to practice. Because I am a follower of Jesus and His Word, my remarks will be based on that perspective. I am going to talk mostly about remarks to audiences, rather than conversations one on one, or among small informal groups. My thoughts can be summarized in three phrases:

"Be Prepared;" "Be Gracious;" and when possible, "Be Brief!"

First, "Be Prepared"
The apostle, Peter, encouraged his listeners,

> ...*Always be prepared to give an answer to everyone who asks you to give the reason for the hope that you have...*
> (1 Peter 3:15)

Communicating clearly is hard work. We have to know our subject, our audience, and the language that can transfer the subject to the audience. One of the great communicators of humor in the twentieth century was Bob Hope. He traveled thousands of miles and visited dozens of military camps to encourage US troops here and overseas. As you listened to his presentations, you realized he prepared diligently. He learned not only the lines for his jokes and humor, but also something about the audience and what they were going through, so he could speak to them about their interests in the language of their culture. As a result, his trips became a legend in the America of his era.

Communicating is a matter of *form* as well as *substance*. Because each of you will need to prepare your own subjects, I want to speak for a moment about the form in which we communicate. One of my older mentors told me, "You can walk with the 'greats.' All you have to do is to take them off the shelf." To me the greatest book on the shelf is the Bible. I studied how Jesus communicated and found He was virtually the only person in the Bible who taught by stories. There are many stories in the Bible, but Jesus was the only one who consistently used stories to communicate. It is these stories (sometimes called "parables"), such as "The Good Samaritan," that we remember so well. Stories are still one of the most effective ways to communicate truth.

I also studied the writings of the Apostle Paul, whose brilliant mind and communication skills were greatly used by God. I found that he often began his messages by identifying with his audience and letting them know he appreciated them.

Then he usually built his case on logic and persuasion, mixed with care and love. It will help you greatly to study the "great communicators."

I urge you to write your messages. If we have enough time, speaking is easy. But it can also become sloppy. It has been said that writing causes us to become "exact." If you want your messages to be well reasoned and orderly, write them before you speak. You can change as needed when you make your presentation, but the basics will be in place.

In addition, writing will preserve your message—for your own future reference, and also for your audience or others who may be interested. Recently, a man related to me an admonition he had received from a friend: "Write for 'shelf-life,'" he was told. Just as food on a supermarket shelf has a "life span," so does our writing. The more carefully it is prepared and packaged, the longer it can last.

Second, "Be Gracious"
The Apostle Paul counseled,

> *Let your speech always be gracious, seasoned with salt,*
> *so that you may know how you ought to answer every one.*
> (Colossians 4:6 RSV)

Communicating is like preparing a meal. I was once warned that some of us communicate in "three course dinners," and some of us do it with "hash"—the same ingredients, but all mixed up and served together! When we communicate, we need to speak graciously, and season our message so it will be well received. I find it best to open with an "appetizer," something that will attract the audience and cause them to want to taste the rest of the presentation. Next give the "meat" of your message. People want and need to be well fed. It is good to make a beautiful presentation, but be sure it has meat in it. Finally, comes the "dessert" or as someone has described it, "the sweet conclusion." I have found the best "dessert" is "hope." I try never to end a message without it.

If I am to be gracious, I must also learn to listen as well as to speak. We are not to "*municate,*" but rather to "*co*-mmunicate"! As one little girl explained to her elderly, incommunicative companion, "First, *I* say a little, and then *you* say a little!" This may be difficult or impossible, when we speak or write publicly. But, we can form the habit of listening and answer graciously if there are questions. And, we can be teachable and listen before we give our message. In fact, we must do this. Most of what I am giving you today came from others. So I need to listen, if I am to have anything to pass on.

There is a tone and a rhythm in language. It is meant to be a graceful melody—not a jumble of sound. But even those of us who do not have melodic voices can be used by God! I personally have a voice that often causes telephone callers to ask, "Is your husband there?" But I felt redeemed one day when a person came up to me after I had spoken to their group and said, "You had a voice that didn't tire me." So I decided that God didn't call me to be a telephone operator. Instead, if I just did what I was born and equipped to do, it would all work out. I believe it will for you, too.

Someone once challenged me, "Why we do something may be the most important question we ask ourselves." I have determined that the best reason for our communications is to glorify God and to help other people, not to glorify us. So, the words we choose are not to "impress," but rather to "express." And they are to make our message clear, not to build up the messenger.

Incidentally, I learned long ago that if I concentrate on myself, and how I may be received, I can experience "stage fright." But if I concentrate on what I am to say, and try and help you succeed in what you are called to be and to do, the fear goes away. You get helped, God gets glorified, and I get to have the fun of being involved.

And speaking of "fun," it usually helps to add a little humor. It relieves the tension for the audience, as well as the presenter, if we can laugh a little as we go along.

Finally, When Possible "Be Brief"
Three thousand years ago, the writer of the Book of Ecclesiastes (who was probably King Solomon) posed a most interesting rhetorical question:

> *The more the words, the less the meaning,*
> *and how does that profit anyone?*
> (Ecclesiastes 6:11 NIV)

Sometimes we need long talks or writings to convey our messages. However, I am becoming more and more convinced that the power of words is often inversely proportional to their number.

At a meeting I attended a few years ago, speakers were asked to give their messages in thirty seconds. One man was cheered after he marched to the microphone and said:

> "To be above with the saints we love,
> Oh! That will be glory!
> But to be below with the saints we know,
> That's another story!"

As we look at the Bible, we see that the "Lord's Prayer" can be recited in about thirty seconds; the "Ten Commandments" in about two minutes; and the "Sermon on the Mount" in about twenty minutes. Innumerable books and articles have been written about each of these, yet the original power-packed documents are very short. The same holds true in more modern times, as we are awed by the brevity of the "Declaration of Independence" and Lincoln's "Gettysburg Address," both of which have become models for those who would learn how to speak and write effectively.

One of the most difficult tasks we faced in getting young lawyers to be effective was to get them to shorten and simplify. When the Apostle Paul was on trial for his life, he set forth his defense as recorded in the twenty-sixth chapter of the Book of Acts in the Bible. His plea can be read in about five minutes. *Yet the Judge was so convicted by his words, that the Judge got up and left the room!*

We also need to avoid speaking or writing too soon. Wait until our thoughts ripen, and then give our conclusions. People usually want to hear solutions, not insoluble problems. I have learned, therefore, to think, question, probe, analyze, and make my conclusions privately, or with a small group, before I present an issue publicly. I am convinced that I have been saved from making some bad mistakes by having to wait, sometimes for years, before I was allowed to speak out publicly on some issue. Also, our writings often improve greatly when we have first honed them through the "give and take" of several verbal presentations.

Now it is time for me to heed my own admonition and ***"Be Brief!"***

As I go, let me give you this final word of encouragement: God has a plan for your life. To find it, reach out and communicate with Him and the people He puts in your path. He will bless you and your endeavors as you walk with Him.

From Grandpa With Love

Part V
Ministering Free of Charge

For you yourselves know how you ought to follow our example. We were not idle when we were with you, nor did we eat anyone's food without paying for it. On the contrary, we worked night and day, laboring and toiling so that we would not be a burden to any of you. We did this, not because we do not have the right to such help, but in order to make ourselves a model for you to follow.
(2 Thessalonians 3:7–9)

Preface

Originally Written in the 1980s

This booklet arose out of a talk I gave many years ago to a small group of believers in a private home. These young men and women were meeting in one of the untold number of unofficial groups led by ordinary lay men and women who gather week after week to study the Bible and share their lives together.

With me was a young seminary-trained Pastor who was also acquainted with the couple who were hosting the study. He listened intently as I discussed the role of ministering free of charge. When the meeting was over and we were leaving, he said forcefully, "You have to put that in writing!"

And I did.

Since that evening, we have discussed this issue with many others over the years. Each time it seems to be a release—not only for other laymen, but also for pastors. Some, of course, were delighted to see ordinary believers join in the good fight. But, after one seminar with pastors, I was surprised, in fact startled, that several of them voiced openly their own thought of leaving the professional ranks to enjoy the freedom of ministering free of charge. An effect that I had not considered nor intended!

But whatever your position or training, I hope these thoughts will encourage you in your own walk with Jesus.

Vocation

As usual, remember we all err. So hold onto what is good (of God)—and discard the rest.

From Grandpa With Love

Ministering Free of Charge

Money and ministry go together. Preachers can't preach, singers can't sing, the naked can't be clothed, the hungry can't be fed, and the sick can't be healed unless someone works and financially supports such ministries for Christ. Although Christians often disagree on doctrinal issues, there is one common area of agreement: Every ministry requires financial support if it is to survive.

The New Testament commends three ways that Christian ministries are to be financially supported. Two are widely preached and practiced. The third option, although described by Paul as a "model" for believers to follow, is seldom discussed or recommended today as a method of financial support.

The first two can be summarized as follows:

First, Financially Supporting Those Who Minister to Us.
The most basic financial support is for those who minister to us as believers. Paul makes it clear this is a legitimate form of earning a livelihood as he states:

> *For the Scripture says,*
> *"Do not muzzle the ox while it is*
> *Treading out the grain."*
> *and "The worker deserves his wages."*
> (1Timothy 5:18)

Such financial support is almost universally recognized and accepted in modern Christian circles. Churches, para-church organizations, and radio and TV ministries all clearly encourage us to support the professional Christian workers who minister to us and feed us as believers. Most, although not all, Christian laypeople have willingly accepted the responsibility of providing financially for the work of the churches and the para-church organizations to which they belong. As institutions grow and the need for additional staff and other expenses increase, there are ever-increasing requests for the members and friends of such organizations to financially support those who minister to them. Despite substantial monetary contributions by the laity, many who engage in such professional Christian service do so at substantial financial sacrifice to themselves and their families.

Second, Financially Supporting Those Who Minister to Others. As we become more mature in our Christian walk, we are urged to see beyond our responsibilities of merely financially supporting those who minister to us and begin to support missionary outreach to others who are as yet unwilling or unable to pay for their own shepherds. The Bible makes it clear that this, too, is a recognized and legitimate use of our financial resources. For example, Paul warmly thanks the church at Philippi:

> ...*for even when I was in Thessalonica,*
> *you sent me aid again and again when I was in need.*
> (Philippians 4:16. See also 2 Corinthians 11:7–9)

Modern churches, para-church organizations, electronic media, and others engaged in various ministries regularly encourage us

Ministering Free of Charge

to give generously so that the Gospel and the love of God may be taken to others. And again, laymen and laywomen have responded generously by contributing vast amounts of money to support such missionary outreaches at home and around the world.

These first two methods of financial support have caused Christian ministry to be compared by some to an athletic contest in which there are "players," "payers," and "prayers." They contend this division of labor has produced vast stands full of Christian spectators who are paying for and praying for a few worn-out players on the field who are attempting to reach the world for Christ. This distinction seems to ignore scripture as set forth by the Apostle Paul as he describes the third method of financial support—i.e.:

Third, Financially Supporting Ourselves So We Can Minister to Others Free of Charge.
1 Corinthians 9 is the clearest and most complete discourse on the privilege of a self-supporting ministry. In verses 1 through 3, Paul sets forth his initial concern, which is also the concern most laypeople face when they think about speaking out for Christ; i.e., that they are not recognized as legitimate by others. As I heard one recognized civic leader say, "I don't like that individual speaking for Christ. If he wanted to talk like that, he should have become a minister."

In verses 4 to 12a and verses 13 and 14, Paul points out (as we have discussed above) that those who do the work of the gospel have the right to receive financial support. But in verse 12b he makes this extraordinary statement:

> *But we did not use this right.*
> *On the contrary, we put up with anything*
> *rather than hinder the gospel of Christ.*

Paul understood, as we understand today, that those who present the claims of Christ may become suspect and "hinder the gospel" if they request financial support from others. By contrast, all of us know the tremendous impact we have when we speak for Christ and serve others without asking for anything in return. Being on a lay "reach out" team, preparing a meal, or repairing a home for the sick or elderly all have enormous effect when they are done free of charge.

In verses 15 to 17, Paul recognizes that we can be tempted to boast when we serve free of charge. Giving can be a tremendous ego builder while receiving can be humbling. Paul wants to make it clear (as we should) that such a self-supporting ministry is not a basis for boasting, but simply an act of obedience to God.

But is there a reward for those who minister, but do not earn their livelihood from such ministry? Paul answers with a resounding, "Yes," as he concludes in verse 18:

> *What then is my reward? Just this: that in preaching the gospel I may offer it free of charge, and so not make use of my rights in preaching it.*

What a luxury! No church boards, no supporters to please. Those who support themselves and minister free of charge are free to report only to God and to those in actual authority over them. Ironically, such self-supporting ministers may be more secure, with more freedom than those who request and receive financial support from others.

In verses 19 to 22, Paul emphasizes that not only is the minister greatly blessed who offers the gospel free of charge, but such a ministry is also a very effective method of reaching others for Christ. Paul states that he became like a Jew to win the Jews. To those not having the law, he became like one not having the law in order to win those not having the law. To the weak, he became weak to win the weak. And then he concludes in verse 22b:

> *"...I have become all things to all men
> so that by all possible means I might save some."*

This is the great power of the common Christian ministry. When we are one with the people to whom we minister, whether it is in the work world where self-supporting ministers spend most of their time (as opposed to professional Christian workers who often spend much of their time within the membership of their Christian organizations) or in some particular subculture or locale in which we are involved, we have a unique and singular opportunity to successfully carry out the work that God has given to us in the portion of the world in which we have been placed (Acts 17:26). Because we are not asking for financial support, we sometimes earn a credibility that cannot be obtained in any other way.

In view of Paul's example and his eloquent statement of the rewards we and others obtain from supporting ourselves rather than receiving financial support from others, why has

Vocation

this method of promoting the gospel not been more widely encouraged and practiced? I think there may be several reasons:

Full Time or Part Time
Neither the Christian professionals nor the laity at large really accept that *all* Christians are called to be "full-time" ministers. Several years ago, an older Christian pastor and author with whom I was visiting called me to account when I referred to my pastor as "*the* minister." Pointing his finger at me, this elder statesman said forcefully, "Don't ever say *the* minister. All Christians are ministers!"

That is the clear teaching of Ephesians 4 in which it is stated that God has called some to be apostles, prophets, evangelists, pastors, and teachers "to equip the saints (all believers) for the work of ministry" (Ephesians 4:11–12 RSV). Despite the fact that this passage is often preached and discussed, the modern church continues, as I did, to call its professional workers "*the* ministers" who are to be supported financially and in prayer by the laity who live and work in the secular world.

Working Two Jobs
It is extremely difficult to carry out the dual functions of a secular occupation and a Christian ministry. Paul knew this was hard and referred repeatedly to the fact that he "worked night and day" so he would not be a burden to those to whom he was ministering. (1 Thessalonians 2:9; 2 Thessalonians 3:8). But Christian laypeople have no monopoly on working night and day. Many individuals in Christian occupations and many others

in secular occupations work long, exhausting hours. However, the more serious difficulty lies in learning two disciplines—one related to the Christian world of the Bible and the other concerning the secular world of computers, medicine, engineering, law, real estate, accounting, construction, etc. Most of us simply do not want to work night and day to learn and to stay proficient in our secular occupation as well as our Biblical calling.

As a result, we prefer to work in the secular world, paying pastors and teachers to feed us and financially supporting missionaries to take the Gospel to others. Or, if we feel particularly spiritual, we may leave our secular world (as many are now doing during their middle years) to go into "full-time professional Christian service" in which we can expect to be financially supported by Christian laymen who stay in the pay-and-pray part of the body of Christ.

Models
There are too few models or examples of self-supporting ministers. There has been a growing group of self-supporting "tentmakers" (named after Paul's secular work (Acts 18:3) gradually emerging on the mission fields to penetrate those countries, which are hostile to professional Christian missionaries. But too few Christian laymen are consciously carrying out, and calling for others to carry out, the privilege of ministering free of charge—without ordination or institutional commission—in the secular world in which each of us lives. Notwithstanding the significant contribution by Christian volunteers, few consciously see themselves as ministers or recognize that they are following the pattern commended by Paul. Rather, they feel frustrated by their dual functions, dreaming of a day when they might *really* minister for Christ as a professional Christian worker.

The Remedy

We need all Christians to minister. This can only happen when all believers acknowledge this fact and the corresponding reality that most of us must financially support our own ministry through our own efforts by working night and day so as not to burden those to whom we minister. The question we must all ask ourselves, then, is this:

> "What needs to be done to help the Biblical concept
> of financially supporting our own ministry
> become a modern-day reality?"

Ministers
The first step is to designate *all* Christians (professional workers *and* laity) as "ministers." Until the church at large utilizes the term "minister" for all those who serve Christ (and after all, the term "minister" simply means "servant"—it is not a title of rank but of action), the uncredentialed, self-disparaging "I'm just a layman" syndrome will be used by Satan to discourage and to make ineffective much of the Body of Christ.

Ministries
Second, we need to see "ministry" as something broader than preaching, singing, or institutional church work. It includes not only those gifted with words, but also those who minister through work. Listen to the admonition of the Apostle Peter:

> *Each one should use whatever gift he has received to serve* (minister to) *others, faithfully administering God's grace in its various forms. If anyone speaks, he should do it as one*

> *speaking the very words of God.
> If anyone serves, he should do it with the strength God provides,
> so that in all things God may be praised through Jesus Christ.
> To him be the glory and the power forever and ever. Amen.*
> (1 Peter 4:10–11)

It is crucial that self-supporting ministers not be seen as engaging in a lower level of ministry beneath paid pastors and financially supported missionaries, *but rather as an exhilarating opportunity by those who voluntarily forego the right to receive financial support in order that they may present the gospel free of charge!*

Equippers

The third step is for full-time Christian workers to be seen by themselves and by others, not as *the* ministers, but as *specially gifted ministers*, many who are to equip other Christian ministers to carry out "the work of the ministry," whatever it may be for each person. One part of such equipping should be to encourage Christians to consider financially supporting their own ministries (as well as supporting other full-time Christian workers at home and on the mission fields of the world) in order that the work of the ministry will be carried on by *all* those who are called to follow Jesus.

Models

Finally, and most difficult, it requires that there be models of effective, self-supporting ministers to encourage both professional Christian workers and Christians at large that this is a legitimate modern-day method of financial support for ministry.

Paul himself modeled this third option for us. He made this clear in his statement to the church at Thessalonica:

> *For you yourselves know how you ought to follow our example. We were not idle when we were with you, nor did we eat anyone's food without paying for it.*
>
> *On the contrary, we worked night and day, laboring and toiling so that we would not be a burden to any of you. We did this, not because we do not have the right to such help, but in order to make ourselves a model for you to follow.*
>
> *For even when we were with you, we gave you this rule: "If a man will not work, he shall not eat."*
> (2 Thessalonians 3:7–10)

One person, while discussing this concept, initially cried out, "But where are the models?"

It is obvious the world needs modern models of self-supporting ministry. Not only must we be open to following Paul's example of self-support when it is appropriate for us, but we must also continually remind others of this option. And, like Paul, we must openly urge them to follow this example when it is appropriate for them.

Conclusion

It is estimated that less than 3 percent of Christians are professional "ministers" or "missionaries." Obviously, this number cannot reach the world for Christ. Instead, it is the task of all Christians to see themselves and all other believers as "ministers" and to recognize that it is through all such ministers that the world will be won for Christ.

At the Lausanne convention in Manila several years ago, Ford Madison, Senior Associate for the Laity, asked the audience of approximately four thousand full-time Christian workers (assembled there from around the world to discuss evangelizing the world for Christ) how they themselves had come to know Jesus Christ. He stated that while traveling for the Lausanne movement to several parts of the world, he had made a simple survey to see who God was using in different countries and wondered what this same survey might show among those assembled in Manila. He first discussed the impact of television and radio celebrities and asked,

"How many of you present here tonight came to Jesus through a TV or radio broadcast? Will you please stand up."

Five to ten percent of the audience stood. Then he recognized the effects of mass evangelism, and asked,

"If you are one of those who came to Christ through mass evangelism, would you stand up?"

Again, five to ten percent stood. Finally, he discussed the impact of the ordinary believers throughout the world and the way in which God used them to bring others to know Jesus and asked,

> "If the one that God used to primarily influence you
> to come to Him was an ordinary layperson,
> would you please stand up?"

With scuffling of chairs and applause and comments, nearly the whole room stood.

> "Keep standing! Look around! This is how God works in our
> world today! This is what we found
> in other countries.
> Just as in Bible times and in every year since Pentecost,
> He uses common people!"

Why are ordinary believers so effective? One basic reason is that they often minister free of charge. When Christians ask for money for themselves or for others, they may be suspect. Improper actions by a few high-profile Christian workers strengthen skeptics' claims that many Christians want others to pay and pray so they can play, not in the athletic sense, but through the ungodly misuse of the funds contributed by others. By contrast, the impact made when Christians minister free of charge, using their own time and financial resources, helps to keep the gospel message pure and our various ministries for Christ believable and sacrificial.

Integrity is a great issue of our time. By extolling the virtue and value of having most Christians minister free of charge, we can help raise up a vast body of believers who see themselves and are seen by others as an unselfish, largely self-supporting army of God dedicated to bringing the gospel free of charge to each of our own worlds. It is hard. It often requires that we work night and day. It requires that we become proficient in secular occupations and also in the Bible or other areas of Christian ministry. But it is an incredible privilege, which God is offering to us as ordinary believers who don't feel called to professional Christian service. *All we have to do is to accept!*

As laymen and laywomen, we have the great privilege of ministering free of charge wherever we are, on Sundays, through Sunday School and church services, and throughout the rest of the week in all the settings where we live and work. We are the church. We are all ministers (servants) of the living God Who we serve by our words and our works every day, all day, wherever we are and whatever we may do. Let's encourage one another to keep at it.

Thank God for the professional Christian workers who strengthen, encourage, console, equip, and up-build us—often a great sacrifice to themselves and their families. *Now let's all continue as full-time servants of Christ to do the work of the ministry to which we are called!*

God's Blessing on You All!

Epilogue

It seems to take a lifetime to learn some of the deepest lessons God is teaching us. It has been true for person after person I have listened to over the years—including a wise old man named Solomon. And it has been true for me!

Many believe Solomon wrote the amorous Song of Solomon as a young man; the wisdom Book of Proverbs in his middle years; and a deeper view of life in Ecclesiastes as he looked back over the years and realized his search for worldly pleasures, possessions, power, and position had been "chasing the wind."

Over and over, he voices his frustrations—and then concludes with this observation in Chapter 12:13:

Now all has been heard:
Here is the conclusion of the matter:
Fear God and keep his commandments,
For this is the whole duty of man.

I decided it was fitting to conclude our study on *Vocation* with the following little poem based on Solomon's conclusion—and mine—that our vocation and life work are so much better when we carry out God's purpose for our lives, rather than *Chasing the Wind.*

See You in Heaven

From Grandpa With Love

Chasing the Wind!

From the Book of Ecclesiastes

The wind blows South, and then it turns North;
Round and round it goes, then returns to its course.
I was chasing the wind, my life was in vain,
As I worked for knowledge, honor, and fame.

I worked night and day, what my eyes saw I had;
I denied myself nothing, but still I felt sad.
For whoever loves money, never gets quite enough,
And appetites get bigger, the more they are stuffed.

Then I learned it was joy, just to work, drink, and eat;
These gifts straight from God, that make our sleep sweet.
True rewards come from Him, when I accept my lot,
So now I thank Him daily, because I am not...,

Chasing, chasing the wind;
What a meaningless way to live.
Chasing, chasing the wind;
Not knowing its God Who can give!

www.ingramcontent.com/pod-product-compliance
Lightning Source LLC
Chambersburg PA
CBHW051804170526
45167CB00005B/1876